The key to keeping up with the pace of change in technology lies in using the cloud, but the key to getting ahead lies in loving the cloud. This book is a great way to start loving the cloud, helping you get ahead of that pace of change.

    – Andy Linham, principal strategy manager, Vodafone

Becoming cloud native is now the standard choice for companies that need to deliver quickly, scale and be competitive. This book clearly lays out strong foundations and ideas from those who've gone before and found a successful path. CTOs and tech teams embarking on the journey to becoming cloud first will benefit from the clarity provided but so will more experienced practitioners looking to be able to explain the concepts more widely.

    – David Espley, CTO, Kaluza

A genuinely comprehensive look at what it means to build and operate in a cloud native world. What makes this book particularly valuable is its understanding that cloud native is as much about business and organisational needs as it is about technology. The case studies powerfully illustrate that real transformation demands a long-term commitment. There's no silver bullet here; instead it dives into the dilemmas, nuances and multiple paths that teams must navigate to solve complex challenges. For anyone looking to understand both the how and the why of cloud native, this is an essential guide.

    – Phil Parker, head of delivery, Equal Experts

A fantastic primer on what cloud native is, what are the critical trade-offs to consider and how you might start with this approach in your organisation. Cloud native is as much organisational as it is technical; the case studies bear witness to this by highlighting the leadership vision they had. If you're considering going cloud native in your company or just curious about what all the fuss is about, start with this book.

    – Jason Brown, GTM incubation, Google Cloud

Everything you have ever wondered about the true value of the cloud, how to scale adoption and why cloud native is so damn complicated is addressed in this fantastic book.

    – Paul McMahon, managing director and head of scaled adoption, engineering and product, Citi

An informative, easy-to-read and simple-to-understand view of the exciting benefits that a cloud rative organisation can hope to achieve and some of the challenges and paths it is possible to take to achieve your goals. As technology and tools change so quickly, this book has some of the latest recommendations. The case studies are particularly interesting to read and help illustrate that no one is standing still in this industry and making mistakes is not a failure. I enjoyed the viewpoint on sustainability which shows what's possible for an organisation that wants to prioritise this and why they might want to do it.

    – Annie Bedford, technical project manager, Citi

A must-read for modern CTOs. Discover how cloud native computing can transform not only your technology, but the way you build, adapt and thrive in a changing world.

    – Guy Sayar, managing director, head of engineering at a global bank

This book is a jewel! It covers extensively all the basics anybody would need to be truly cloud native and gives real-world examples of all this knowledge applied in different businesses in a very pragmatic manner. A must-read for anyone who wants to truly embrace the full potential of the cloud.

    – Marc Cluet, executive director, core platform engineering, UBS and London DevOps organiser

THE
CLOUD
NATIVE
ATTITUDE

How the world's best companies use
the cloud to speed up, scale up and
find product market fit

Anne Currie
with Jamie Dobson

The Cloud Native Attitude
ISBN 978-1-915483-79-9 (paperback)
ISBN 978-1-915483-80-5 (ebook)

Published in 2025 by Right Book Press
Printed in the UK

Contents

Foreword

When I first met Anne and Jamie in 2016, I was navigating the then-burgeoning cloud native scene – a complex, rapidly evolving landscape that demanded both technical acumen and organisational insight. What struck me immediately was their rare ability to see the bigger picture: the interplay of technology, culture and attitude that would determine success in this new paradigm. At the time, I was working for a tier 1 bank on a company-wide OpenShift (Kubernetes) platform. Anne and Jamie's ability to articulate challenges that extended beyond the merely technical resonated deeply with my experience. It was no surprise that they both were associated with a trialblazing company devoted to solving these technical and organisational challenges holistically.

Jamie founded Container Solutions in 2014, driven by a clear vision: to help organisations embrace a fundamental shift in 'attitude' that would unlock the full potential of cloud services and cloud native technologies. Anne, a long-time associate and thought leader in the field, not to mention a long-running collaborator with Jamie, has been instrumental in shaping and communicating these ideas, enabling businesses to succeed in their cloud native journeys.

Their message remains as vital today as it was a decade ago. As part of their work, Anne and Jamie are still visiting clients who often still believe their struggles are rooted in technology when, in fact, they stem from deeper challenges: cultural inertia, outdated mindsets and the inability to adapt to new ways of working. This ongoing relevance is reflected in the rapid growth of cloud adoption. Between 2015 and 2022, the proportion of corporate data stored in the cloud more than doubled, from 30 to 60 per cent. Such growth underscores the urgency for businesses to move beyond technology and address the attitudes required for transformation.

This book distils Anne and Jamie's years of experience into a comprehensive guide to cloud native success. It goes beyond the buzzwords to explain the key ingredients necessary to deliver on the promise of speed, scale and margin. These principles are illustrated through real-world examples drawn from Container Solutions' consulting work.

Beyond their consulting work, Jamie and the team at Container Solutions have contributed significantly to the broader community through projects like the External Secrets Operator (external-secrets.io) and the Java Kubernetes SDK (developers.redhat.com/articles/2022/02/15/write-kuber-netes-java-java-operator-sdk). They also developed Cloud Native Patterns, an open-source framework that equips organisations with a shared language to address their challenges (cnpatterns.org).

The Cloud Native Attitude builds on these contributions to offer something unique: not just a theoretical exploration of cloud native, but a deeply practical guide grounded in lived experience. Through case studies that span the history of cloud native practice – ranging from cloud-born companies like Starling Bank and cinch to transformative journeys at legacy organisations like the *Financial Times* – the book shows how cloud native implementation has evolved and how businesses can adapt to the challenges they face today.

I joined Container Solutions in 2020 as a cloud native consultant, and it has been a privilege to witness first hand the challenges and triumphs of businesses as they embrace cloud native technologies. This book captures that journey, offering not just insights into what it takes to succeed, but also reassurance that the challenges you face are shared by many – and that they can be overcome.

As you read, I hope you'll find practical wisdom and fresh perspectives that will inspire and equip you for your own cloud native transformation. The road may be complex, but with the right attitude, the possibilities are imitless.

Ian Miell

Introduction

This is a small book with a single purpose – to tell you all about cloud native computing (hereafter, we'll just call it cloud native): what it is, what it's for, who's using it and why. Go to any software conference and you'll hear endless discussions about containers, orchestrators and microservices. Why are they so fashionable? Are there good reasons for using them? What are the trade-offs, and do you have to take a big-bang approach to adoption? We step back from the hype, summarise the key concepts and interview some of the enterprises that have adopted cloud native in production.

Take copies of this book and pass them around, or just zoom in to increase the text size on the ebook version and ask your colleagues to read over your shoulder.

The only hard thing about this book s that you can't assume anyone else has read it.

What on earth is cloud native?

According to the Cloud Native Computing Foundation (CNCF), cloud native is about scale and resilience or 'distributed systems capable of scaling to tens of thousands of self-healing multi-tenant nodes'.

This sounds great for companies like Uber or Netflix that want to hyperscale an existing product and control their operating costs. But is a cloud native approach just about power and scale? Is it of any use to enterprises of more normal dimensions? What about people who just want to get new products and services to market faster, like those at the UK's *Financial Times?* Ten years ago they were looking for an architectural approach that would let them innovate more rapidly. Did cloud native deliver speed for them? Start-ups want to create and test new business ideas without large capital expenditure, starting small with minimal costs. So, is cloud native just a way to reduce bills?

Why does this book even exist?

When we wrote the first edition of this book back in 2017, we wanted to understand what cloud native was actually being used for, what it could deliver in reality and what the trade-offs and downsides were.

We interviewed a range of companies that had adopted a cloud native approach because we wanted to understand what they had learned. These were companies such as the flight booking unicorn Skyscanner, the global newspaper the *Financial Times* and UK challenger bank Starling. We've also built and operated systems ourselves for more than 20 years and many of the brand-new ideas coming out of cloud native seemed oddly familiar.

Since then, we've helped a huge range of our clients adopt a cloud native approach, and a large number of books have been published that explore the topic. *Accelerate*, by Nicole Forsgren, Jez Humble and Gene Kim (2018), helped to explain why techniques such as continuous delivery are so effective; *Team Topologies*, by Matthew Skelton and Manuel Pais (2019), helped to codify how teams could be structured to support the new cloud native approach; and *Cloud Native Transformation*, by Pini Reznik and Jamie Dobson along with Michelle Gienow (2019), provided a practical guide for how to get there.

The third edition of this book is a distillation of what we gleaned from our conversations with users, vendors, hosting providers, journalists, researchers and our own clients, updated to reflect what has changed in the seven years since the first edition came out. The book made us ask ourselves, what the heck is cloud native? Is it a way to move faster? A powerful way to scale? A way to reduce operational costs or capital expenditure? How can these different aims be achieved with one paradigm? Finally, is it good that cloud native can potentially do so much, or is that a risk?

With everyone from the ordinary developer to the chief technology officer (CTO) in mind, this book explores cloud native's multiple meanings and tries to cut through the waffle to identify the right cloud native strategy for specific needs. We argue that moving fast, being scalable and reducing costs are all achievable with a cloud native approach, but they need careful thought. Cloud native has huge potential, but it also has its dangers.

Finally, we reflect on what cloud native really means. Is it a system of rules or more of a frame of mind? Is it the opposite of waterfall or the opposite of agile? Or are those both utterly meaningless questions?

What is cloud native?

Cloud native is the name of a particular approach to designing, building and running applications based on the cloud (infrastructure as a service, IaaS) or platform as a service (PaaS). In the first edition of this book, we argued that being cloud native was also tightly tied to using a microservice architecture, and for much of 2019 and 2020 the Cloud Native Computing Foundation's definition of cloud native agreed with us. Since then, however, the CNCF definition has softened its language around microservices, reflecting the fact that the pendulum seems to be swinging back a little towards monoliths as more organisations discover the trade-offs, particularly around operational complexity, that come with a microservices architecture. (If any of these terms are unfamiliar to you, we've provided a glossary at the end of the book.)

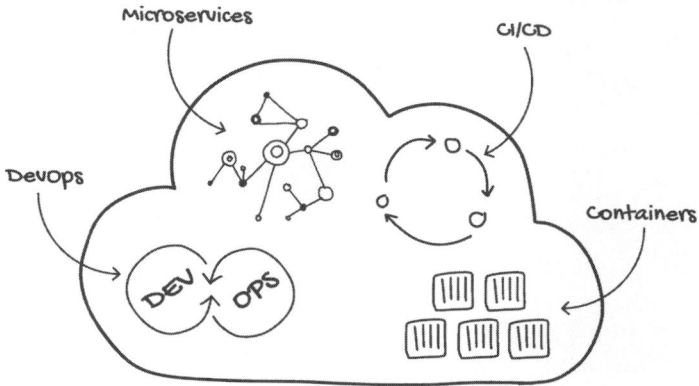

Likewise, in our first edition, we suggested that a cloud native approach relied on containers and orchestrators such as Kubernetes. While this remains by far the most popular approach, the rise of serverless options, and particularly function as a service (FaaS) offerings such as Amazon Web Services' Lambda and Azure functions, does offer an alternative that can support a surprisingly wide range of use cases, from the BBC's iPlayer to Honeycomb's data read/write layer, as well as the more obvious ecommerce use cases such as second-hand car start-up cinch, which we meet later in the book. It should be said that under the hood, all the FaaS implementations we're aware of make use of some sort of container-ish technology, but this is sufficiently abstracted away from the developer that you are not particularly aware of it.

What hasn't changed is that the overall objective of a cloud native approach is to improve speed, scalability and finally margin.

Speed

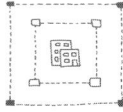
Scale

Margin

Speed: Companies of all sizes now see strategic advantage in being able to innovate quickly and get ideas to market fast. By this we mean moving from months to get an idea into production to days or even hours. Key to achieving this is a cultural shift within a business: transitioning from big-bang projects to more incremental improvements. Part of it is also about managing risk. While Facebook founder Mark Zuckerberg infamously suggested we should 'move fast and break things', we believe that, at its best, a cloud native approach is about de-risking as well as accelerating change, allowing companies to delegate more aggressively and thus become more responsive. In this context, speed is measured not merely in terms of the number of features you can ship per hour or day, but also in terms of the number you can ship while maintaining a highly available service.

Scale: As businesses grow, it becomes strategically necessary to support more users, in more locations, with a broader range of devices, while maintaining responsiveness, managing costs and not falling over.

Margin: In the new world of cloud infrastructure, a strategic goal may be to pay for additional resources only as they're needed, eg as new customers come online. Spending moves from upfront capital expenditure (buying new machines in anticipation of success) to operational expenditure (paying for additional servers on demand). But this is not all. Machines can be bought just in time but that doesn't mean they're being used efficiently. Another stage in cloud native is usually to spend less on hosting.

At its heart, a cloud native strategy is about handling technical risk. In the past, the standard approach to avoiding danger was to move slowly and carefully. The cloud native approach is about moving quickly by taking small, reversible and low-risk steps. This can be extremely powerful, but it isn't free, and it isn't easy. It's a huge philosophical and cultural shift as well as a technical challenge.

How does cloud native work?

The fundamentals of cloud native have been described as container packaging, dynamic management and a microservices-oriented architecture, which all sounds like a lot of work. What does cloud native actually mean and is it worth the effort?

We believe that cloud native is all about five architectural principles:

- ↪ **Use infrastructure or platform as a service**: Run on compute resources that can be flexibly provisioned on demand. These may still be in house, and we are even seeing some cases where firms are moving from public cloud offerings back to their own data centres. It's only a small number, but we may see more of this in future – or not. Most commonly, however, these resources are provided by public cloud providers such as Amazon Web Services (AWS), Microsoft Azure, Google Cloud Platform (GCP), DigitalOcean or Alibaba Cloud.

- ↪ **Design systems using, or evolve them towards, a microservices architecture**: Prioritise individual components that are small and decoupled, meaning, crucially, that they are also independently deployable.

- ↪ **Automate and encode**: Replace manual tasks with scripts or code – for example, using automated test suites, configuration tools and continuous integration (CI) or continuous delivery (CD).

↳ **Containerise**: Package processes together with their dependencies, making them easy to test, move and deploy.

↳ **Orchestrate**: Abstract away individual servers in production using off-the-shelf dynamic management and orchestration tools.

These steps have many benefits, but ultimately they are about the reduction of risk. More than a decade ago when working for a small enterprise, one of us lay awake at night wondering what was actually running on the production servers, whether they could be reproduced and how reliant the team were on individuals and their ability to cross a busy street. It was worrying to think about whether there was enough hardware for the current big project. These were the most unrecoverable risks. Finally, deployments breaking the existing services, which were tied together like strings of spaghetti, was a worry, too. All this worrying didn't leave much time for imaginative ideas about the future (or sleep).

In that world before the cloud, infrastructure as code (scripted environment creation), automated testing, containerisation and microservices, we had no choice but to move slowly, spending lots of time on planning, testing and documentation. That was absolutely the right thing to do then to control technical risk. However, the question now is, 'Is moving slowly our only option?' In fact, is it even the safest option anymore?

We're not considering the cloud native approach because it's fashionable, although it remains the case that it is. We have a pragmatic motivation: the approach appears to work well with continuous delivery, provide faster time to value (TTV), scale well and be efficient to operate. However, most importantly it seems to help reduce risk in a new way, by going fast but small. It's that practical reasoning we'll be evaluating in the rest of this book.

1 The cloud native quest

In our introduction, we defined cloud native as a set of tools for helping with three major objectives:

1. **Speed**: Faster delivery for products and features (aka feature velocity or TTV).
2. **Scale**: Maintaining performance while serving more users.
3. **Margin**: Minimising infrastructure and people bills.

We also suggested that cloud native strategies have a focus on infrastructure:

↳ Start with a cloud (IaaS or PaaS) infrastructure.
↳ Leverage new architectural concepts that have infrastructural impact (microservices or FaaS).
↳ Use open-source infrastructure tools (orchestrators and containers).

We believe that cloud native is a technique that marries application architecture and operational architecture, and that makes it particularly interesting.

In this chapter, we're going to talk about the goals we're trying to achieve with cloud native: going faster, bigger and cheaper.

The goals of speed, scale and margin

First of all, let's define what we mean by these objectives in this context. Nearly two decades into the availability of public cloud platforms, it remains the case that the most common desire we're seeing from businesses is for speed – so that's where we'll start.

Speed

In the cloud native world, we're defining speed as TTV: the elapsed clock time between a valid idea being generated and becoming a product or feature that users can see, use and hopefully pay for. But value doesn't only mean revenue. For some start-ups, value may lie in user numbers or votes. It's whatever the business chooses to care about.

We've used the phrase 'clock time' to differentiate between a feature that takes three 'person days' to deliver but launches tomorrow, and a feature that takes one person day but launches in two months' time. The goal we're talking about here is how to launch sooner rather than how to minimise engineer hours.

Scale

We all know you can deliver a prototype that supports 100 users far more quickly, easily and cheaply than a fully resilient product supporting 100,000. Launching prototypes that don't scale well is a sensible approach when you don't yet know if a product or feature has appeal. There's no point in over-engineering it. However, the point of launching prototypes is to find a product that will eventually need to support those 100,000 users and many more. When this happens, your problem becomes scale: how to support more customers in more locations while providing the same or a better level of service. Ideally, we don't want to have to expensively and time-consumingly rewrite products from scratch to handle success (although in some cases that's the right call).

Margin

It's easy to spend money in the cloud. That's not always a bad thing. Many start-ups and scale-ups rely on the fact that it's fast and straightforward to acquire more compute resources just by getting out a credit card. That wasn't an option 15 years ago.

However, the time eventually comes when people want to stop giving AWS, Microsoft or Google a big chunk of their profits. At that point, their problem becomes how to maintain existing speed and service levels while significantly cutting operational costs.

What type of business do you have?

Before we jump into choosing an objective, let's consider that a goal is of no use unless it's addressing a problem you actually have, and that different companies in different stages of their development usually have different problems.

Throughout this book, we'll be talking about the kinds of businesses that choose a cloud native strategy. Every business is different, but to keep things simple, we're going to generalise to three company types that each represent a different set of problems: the start-up, the scale-up and the enterprise.

The start-up

A start-up in this context is any company that's experimenting with a business model and trying to find the right combination of product, licence, customers and channels. A start-up is a business in an exploratory phase, trying and discarding new features and hopefully growing its user base.

Avoiding risky upfront capital expenditure is the first issue, but that's fairly easily resolved by building in the cloud. Next, speed of iteration becomes the problem, testing out various models as rapidly as possible to see what works. Scale and margin are not yet critical problems for a start-up.

A start-up doesn't have to be new. Groups within a larger

enterprise may act like start-ups when they're investigating new products and want to learn quickly.

There's an implication here that the business is able to experiment with its business model. That's easy for internet products and much harder for hardware or on-premises products. For the speed aspect of cloud native, we're primarily describing benefits only available to companies selling software they can update at will. If you can't update your end product, continuous integration or delivery doesn't buy you as much, although it can still be of use.

The scale-up

A scale-up is a business that needs to grow fast and have its systems grow alongside it. It has to support more users in more geographic regions on more devices. Suddenly its problem is scale. It wants size, resilience and response times. Scale is not just about how many users you can support. You might be able to handle 100 times the users if you accept falling over a lot, but we wouldn't call that proper scaling. Similarly, if you handle the users but your system becomes terribly slow, that isn't successful scaling either. A scale-up wants more users with the same or better service-level agreement (SLA) and response times, and doesn't want to massively increase the size of its operations and support teams to achieve it.

the start-up   the scale-up   the enterprise

The enterprise

Finally, we have the grown-up business: the enterprise. This company may have one or many mature products at scale. It will still be wrestling with speed and scale but margin is also now a concern: how to grow its customer base for existing products while remaining profitable. It no longer wants to move quickly or scale by just throwing money at the problem. It's worried about its overall hosting bills and cost per user. Being big, resilient and fast is no longer enough. It also wants to be cost effective.

Where to start?

It's a good idea to pursue any wide-ranging objective such as speed, scale or margin in small steps with clear wins. For example, pursue faster feature delivery for one product first. Then, when you're happy with your progress and delivery, apply what you've learned to other products.

It's a dangerous idea to pursue multiple objectives of cloud native simultaneously. It's too hard. Every cloud native project is challenging and, as we'll read in our case studies, it requires focus and commitment. Don't fight a war on more than one front.

Your objectives don't have to be extreme. Company A might be happy to decrease its deployment time from three months to three days. For Company B, its objective will only be achieved when it can deploy as often as required, multiple times per day. Neither Company A nor Company B is wrong – as long as they've chosen the right target for their own business. When it comes to 'define your goal', the operative word is 'your'.

So, to sum up, if you're searching for product fit, you're in start-up mode and are probably most interested in speed of iteration and feature velocity. If you have a product that needs to support many more users, you may be in scale-up mode and you're interested in handling more requests from new locations while maintaining availability and response times. Finally, if you're now looking to maximise your profitability, you're in enterprise mode and interested in cutting your hosting and operational costs without losing any of the speed and scalability benefits you've already accrued.

OK, that all sounds reasonable! In the next chapter, we're going to start looking at the tools we can use to get there.

2 Do containers have it all wrapped up?

In the last chapter, we described the cloud native goals of speed, scale and margin, or going faster, bigger and cheaper. Next, we're going to look at some of the tools that cloud native uses to tackle these goals, including container packaging, dynamic management and a microservices-oriented architecture.

In this chapter, we'll consider container packaging: what it is and the effect it has. But first, let's take a big step back. What are we running on?

IaaS, PaaS or your own data centre?

Before we start talking about software and tools, a good question is, where is all this stuff running? Does cloud native have to be in the cloud? Crucially, does a cloud native strategy have to use infrastructure as a service (IaaS) or platform as a service (PaaS) with the physical machines owned and managed by a supplier such as Microsoft, Google or AWS? Or could you build your own servers and infrastructure?

We'd argue that cloud native strategies fundamentally exploit the risk-reduction advantages of IaaS or PaaS. These include:

↳ very fast access to flexible, virtual resources (expand or contract your estate at will), which changes infrastructure planning from high to low risk

↳ lower cost of entry and exit for projects – the transition from CAPEX (capital expenditure, ie buying a lot of machines upfront) to OPEX (operating expenses, ie hiring machines short term as needed) de-risks project strategy by minimising sunk costs and making course corrections or full strategy shifts easier

↳ access to cloud-hosted, managed services (such as databases as a service, load balancers and firewalls, as well as specialist services such as data analytics or machine learning) makes it faster and easier to develop more sophisticated new products, which can help identify opportunities more quickly and reduce the risks of experimentation.

These advantages can potentially be duplicated by a large organisation in its own data centres: Google, Facebook and others have done so. However, it's difficult, distracting, time consuming and costly. Therefore it's a risky process. For many enterprises, it's more efficient to buy these IaaS/ PaaS advantages off the shelf from a cloud provider. If you have a tech team smart enough to build a private cloud as well as Google or AWS, is that the best way for your business to use them?

So, cloud native systems don't have to run in the cloud, but cloud native does have tough prerequisites that are already met by many cloud providers and are increasingly commoditised and difficult to build internally. To be honest, we'd probably use the cloud unless we were Google.

Containers

In the cloud native vision, applications are supplied, deployed and run in something called a container. This is just the word we use to describe cleverly wrapping up all the processes and libraries we need to run a particular application into a single package and putting an interface on t to help us move it about. The original and most popular tool for creating these containerised applications was Docker.

Since we published the first edition of this book, containers have become ubiquitous. This happened because they accomplished four incredibly sensible things:

↳ **A standard packaging format**: Docker invented a simple and popular packaging format that wrapped an application and all its dependencies into a single blob and was consistent across all operating systems. This common format encouraged other companies and lots of start-ups to develop new tools for creating, scanning and manipulating containerised applications. Docker's format is now the de facto standard for containerised application packaging. Its containerised application packages or 'images' are used on most operating systems with a wide set of build, deployment and operational tools from a variety of vendors. The image format and its implementation are both open source. In addition, Docker's container images are 'immutable': once they're running, you can't change or patch them. That also turns out to be a very handy feature from a security perspective.

↳ **Lightweight application isolation without a virtual machine (VM)**: A 'container engine' like Docker's Engine, CoreOS's rkt (pronounced rocket), runC, CRI-O or, for Windows Server users, Windows Containers, is required to run a containerised application package (aka an 'image') on a machine.

However, an engine does more than just unpack and execute packaged processes. When a container engine runs an application image, it limits what the running app can see and do on the machine. A container engine can ensure that applications don't interfere with one another by either overwriting vital libraries or competing for resources. The engine also allows different versions of the same library to be used by different containers on the host. A running containerised application behaves a bit like an app running in a very simple virtual machine, but it's not one: the isolation is applied by the container engine process but enforced directly by the host kernel. A container image once running is referred to as just a 'container' and it's transient – unlike a VM, a container only exists while it's executing (after all, it's just a process with some additional limitations being enforced by the kernel). Also, unlike a heavyweight VM, a container can start and stop very quickly – in seconds. We call this potential for quick creation and destruction of containers 'fast instantiation' and it's fundamental to dynamic management. Most modern container engines use the Open Container Initiative (OCI) container image format. OCI container images are a representation of a container and the software that should run within it, making it possible to create new containers in a predictable, repeatable way.

↳ **A standard application control interface**: Just as importantly, a container engine also provides a standard interface for controlling running containers. This means third-party tools can start and stop containerised applications or change the resources assigned to them. The concept of a common control interface for any application running on any operating system is surprisingly radical and is, again, vital to dynamic management.

↳ **Immutable infrastructure**: Historically, computers and software systems have been treated as mutable infrastructure, with changes applied to an existing system either all at once or over a period of time. While working for a UK retail bank in the early 2000s, one of us spent many painful hours installing software on the four clustered Windows servers that were to run a new internet banking system. The machines needed to be identical, down to the exact order in which software and patches were installed, since one piece of software would replace older binaries and make incremental updates to configuration files. Individual configuration files also had to be updated by hand. The process was absurdly hard and error prone. In an immutable system, rather than a series of incremental updates and changes, an entirely new complete image is built, and the update replaces the entire image with a newer one in a single operation. There are no incremental changes. Additionally, building a new image means the old one is still around and can be quickly used for a rollback if something goes wrong.

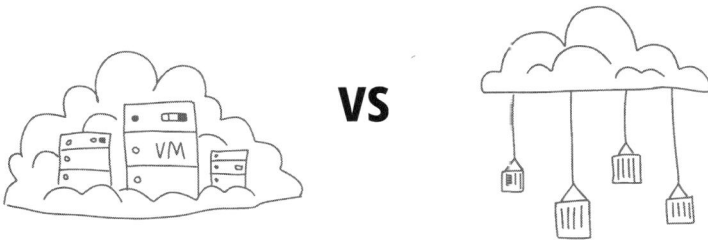

Together, these four revolutionary innovations have changed our assumptions about how data centres can be operated and, crucially, about how rapidly new applications can be deployed.

Alternatives to containers

As you scale up your deployments, you find that the key to running containers at scale is orchestration. At a minimum, an orchestrator gives you the ability to place containers, migrate them if the host fails, and provide additional services such as configuration management, network configuration and storage. Kubernetes (K8s) is the mass-market leader and is the natural default choice. We'll explore orchestrators in more detail in the next chapter, but before we do, we should think about what other options we have.

Once the concepts of standardised application packaging, isolation and control were out there, alternative approaches were developed to provide some of the same functionality. Unikernels and lighter-weight VMs remain options, but at this point the only alternative that can approach the level of hype that containers and Kubernetes enjoy are serverless or FaaS options such as AWS Lambda, Azure Functions or Google Cloud Functions.

Likewise, other container types similar to Docker exist, and even more ways to achieve the benefits of containers will undoubtedly be developed. However, what's important is understanding the advantages of common packaging, control interfaces and application isolation even if, in five years' time, we end up using something other than containers to provide these features.

A quick aside: to avoid confusion, although the interface for managing Docker images is consistent across all operating systems, the contents of an image are not necessarily portable. The contents of a container image are a set of executables. A Linux container image will only include executables compiled to run on Linux. A Windows image will only include executables (EXEs) and dynamic link libraries (DLLs) compiled to run on Windows. You therefore can't run a Linux container image on Windows or a Windows container image on Linux, any more than you can run an executable compiled for one on the other. However, once the containers are running on the right host operating system (OS), you can control them all with the same format of application programming interface (API) calls. Remember, the container engine is not a runtime environment like Java. Containers run natively on the host so the executables must be compiled for that OS.

Is a container as good as a VM?

Before we get too carried away, there are still ways in which a VM is better than a container. On the downside:

↳ VMs need more memory than a container.

↳ VMs consume more host machine resources to run than containers.

↳ VMs take much longer to start and stop (minutes vs seconds).

In the VM's favour, however, it's a much more mature technology with years of tooling behind it. Also, containers isolate processes but at the moment they don't do it perfectly and can be hacked. The VMs are currently more secure.

Why is everyone mad about containers anyway?

The reason everyone's still crazy about containers is not just because they're a nice packaging format that plays well with automated deployments. Containers also provide us with lightweight application isolation and a standard application control API paired with dynamic management that can give us automation, resilience and much better resource utilisation, making containers potentially greener and cheaper. But more on that in the next chapter.

3 Is dynamic management the prime mover?

Dynamic infrastructure management is sometimes described as programmable infrastructure and its purpose is to automate data centre tasks previously done by operations (ops) people. This potentially has multiple benefits:

↳ improved ops team productivity
↳ systems that can react faster and more consistently to failure or attack and are therefore more resilient
↳ systems that can have more component parts (eg be bigger)
↳ systems that can manage their resources more efficiently and therefore be cheaper to operate.

Dynamic management relies on an operational tool called a container orchestrator.

What is an orchestrator?

According to Wikipedia, orchestration s the automated arrangement, coordination and management of computer systems.

Orchestration tools for controlling VMs running on physical servers have been around a long time. VM orchestrators underpin the modern cloud: they allow cloud providers to pack many VMs efficiently onto huge servers and manage them there. Without that, operating the cloud would cost too much. However, container orchestrators can do even more than VM orchestrators.

Container orchestrators

Container orchestrators such as Kubernetes or Nomad remotely control containers running on any machine within a defined set called a cluster. Among other things, these orchestrators dynamically manage the cluster to automatically spot and restart failed applications (aka fault tolerance) and ensure the resources of the cluster are being used efficiently (aka bin packing).

The basic idea of any orchestrator (VM or container) is that we puny humans don't need to control individual machines; we can just set high-level directives and let the orchestrator worry about what's happening on any particular server.

We mentioned in the last chapter that containers are lightweight compared to VMs; they are also highly transient (they may only exist for seconds or minutes). We're already dependent on VM orchestrators to operate virtualised data centres because there are so many VMs. Within a containerised data centre there will be more containers to many orders of magnitude. Google, one of the earliest users of container technology in production, starts more than two billion containers every week. Most cf us aren't going to do that (!), but if we don't operate many more containers than we currently do VMs, then we're missing out. Container orchestrators will almost certainly be required to manage these greater numbers effectively.

Is dynamic management just orchestration?

Right now, dynamic management is mostly what we can do out of the box with orchestrators (better resource utilisation and automated resilience), although even that entry-level functionality is extremely useful. However, orchestrators also let third parties write tools to control the containers under the orchestrator's management. In future, these tools will do even more useful things, such as improve security and energy consumption. We know of at least one small company that has cut some hosting bills by 70 per cent using a container orchestrator and its own custom tools in production.

Automation

The purpose of dynamic management is to automate data centres. We can do that with conta ner orchestrators because of our four revolutionary features of containers:

- ↳ a standard application packaging format
- ↳ a lightweight application isolation mechanism
- ↳ a standard application control interface
- ↳ immutable infrastructure.

We've never had these features in a commonly adopted form (Docker-compatible containers in this case) before, but with them we can quickly, safely and programmatically move applications from place to place and co-locate them. Data centres can be operated:

- ↳ at greater scale
- ↳ more efficiently (in terms of resources)
- ↳ more productively (in terms of manpower)
- ↳ more securely.

Orchestrators play a key role in delivering the cloud native goals of scale and margin but can also be useful in helping to automate deployment, which can in turn improve feature velocity.

Choosing an orchestrator

Kubernetes requires significant time and deep understanding to deploy, operate and troubleshoot. Because of this, if you're running your workloads on a public cloud it generally makes sense to choose a managed Kubernetes service from one of the major cloud vendors such as Microsoft's Azure Kubernetes Service (AKS), Amazon Elastic Kubernetes Service (EKS) or Google Kubernetes Engine (GKE).

For enterprises that are using a hybrid cloud approach or on-premises (on-prem), a Kubernetes distribution such as Red Hat's OpenShift is a good option, and adds a number of additional capabilities on top of what Kubernetes already provides, including routing traffic to your web service from the outside world via the OpenShift router.

Of the direct competitors to Kubernetes, Hashicorp's Nomad has a very flexible model for running different sorts of application workloads, including Java applications, VMs, Hadoop jobs and so on, and allows for a great deal of customisation. It also works well with the other members of the Hashicorp stack (Vault and Consul) so, while it may not be a mass-market competitor, it may well be worth a look if you want this kind of flexibility.

Finally, if your particular use cases allow, it may be

possible to skip Kubernetes and containers altogether, going instead for FaaS options such as AWS Lambda, Azure Functions or Google Cloud Functions, or PaaS options such as Heroku, Platform.sh or Railway. Heroku really set the benchmark for developer productivity but unfortunately it hasn't evolved much since Salesforce acquired it in 2010. That said, if your application can fit into the given platform constraints, a PaaS might well be a productive option.

Sounds marvellous. Is there a catch?

As we've discussed, dynamic management relies on container features such as very fast instantiation speeds: seconds or sub-seconds compared to minutes for VMs. Tools designed for working with applications running in VMs may not respond quickly enough to handle dynamically managed containers. For example, it's worth checking that your firewalls and load balancers can handle applications that appear and disappear in seconds. The same is true of service discovery, logging and monitoring services. Input/output (I/O) operations can also be a problem for extremely short-lived processes.

These issues have been addressed by modern products that are container friendly, but companies may have to move away from some old familiar tools to newer ones to be able to use dynamic management. Unfortunately, the newer products, such as service meshes, can be complex to manage and resource intensive. It often makes sense in a container world to hold state in managed stateful services (see Chapter 4) such as databases as a service rather than to battle the requirements of fast I/O. Similarly, choosing a managed PaaS with built-in service discovery (eg AWS Lambda) could make your life easier than wrestling with your own service mesh.

Which came first, the container or the orchestrator?

Companies that start by running containers in production often move on to using orchestrators because they can save so much hosting money. Many early container adopters such as the *Financial Times* or the internet bank Starling initially wrote their own orchestrators but later adopted off-the-shelf versions like Kubernetes as those commercial products became more mature.

So, is the first step in a cloud native strategy always to adopt containers, quickly followed by orchestrators? Actually, not necessarily. Many companies start with microservices, as we'll see in the next chapter.

4 Microservices: the killer horde?

In the previous chapters, we talked about two of the architectural and operational weapons of cloud native: containers and dynamic management. However, when we go out and speak to experienced cloud native users, we find that containers and orchestrators aren't always where they started. Many companies begin with microservices and don't adopt containers until later.

In this chapter, we're going to look at microservices-oriented architectures and think about how they fit in with the other cloud native tools.

Microservices architectures

The microservice concept is a deceptively simple one. Complex, multipurpose applications (aka monoliths) are broken down into small, single-purpose and self-contained services that are decoupled and communicate with one another via well-defined messages.

In theory, the motivation is threefold. Microservices are potentially:

↳ easier to develop and update
↳ more robust and scalable
↳ cheaper to operate and support.

However, these benefits are not trivial to deliver. Architecting microservices is a difficult thing to get your head around. Microservices can achieve several competing objectives and it's important to think carefully about what your initial goal is or you could end up with a mess.

Let's talk about state

Let's briefly step back and discuss something that often comes up when we're talking about microservices: state. There are broadly two types of microservice: 'stateless' and 'stateful'.

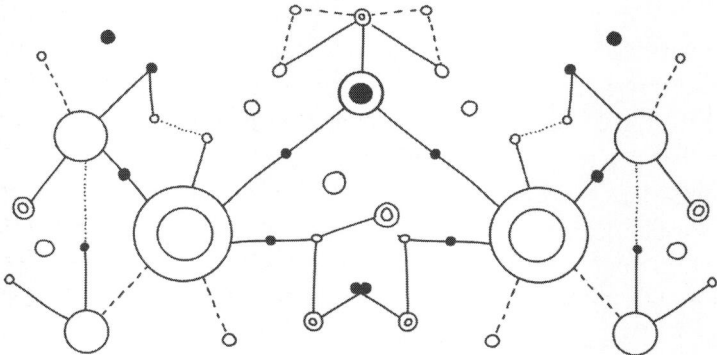

Stateful microservices possess saved data in a database that they read from and write to directly. Note that when a stateful service terminates, it has to save its state. Well-behaved stateful microservices don't tend to share databases with other microservices because that makes it hard to maintain decoupling and well-defined interfaces.

Stateless microservices handle requests and return responses. Everything they need to know is supplied on the request and, once the request is complete, they forget it. They don't keep any permanent notes to remind them where they got to. When a stateless service terminates, it has nothing to save. It may not complete a request, but c'est la vie – that's the caller's problem.

The point of microservices

We have already discussed how cloud native has three potential goals: speed, scale and margin. To optimise for each of these, you might design your microservices architecture differently.

Microservices for speed (feature velocity)

A very common motivation for moving to a microservices architecture is to make life easier for your tech teams. If you have a large team all working on the same big codebase, then that can cause clashes and merge conflicts and there's a lot of code for everyone to understand. So, it would instantly seem easier if every service was smaller and separated by a clear interface. That way, each microservice can be owned by a small team who'll all work together happily, so long as they like the same pizza toppings. Teams can then safely deploy changes at will without having to even talk to those four cheeses down the hall, as long as no fool changes the API...

Microservices for scale

In the past, you'd spend $5 million on a mainframe and it would run for ten years with no downtime. Mainframes are the classic example of vertical scaling, with all its strengths and weaknesses. We wouldn't recommend a mainframe for many reasons, but three particularly leap to mind:

↳ Any one machine will eventually run out of capacity.
↳ A single machine can only be in one place: it can't provide fast response times for users all over the world.
↳ They are hard to manage and maintain.

31

If you want to scale forever, or you have geographically dispersed users, you may prefer to architect for horizontal scaling, ie lots of distributed small machines rather than one big one.

Basically, for horizontal scaling you want to be able to start more copies of your application to support more users. The self-contained nature of microservices works well with this: an individual instance of a microservice is generally decoupled not only from other microservices but also from other instances of itself, so you can safely start lots and lots of copies. That effectively gives you instant horizontal scaling. How great is that?

Actually, it gets even better. If you have lots of copies of your application running for scale that can also provide resilience; if one falls over you just start up another. You can even automate this if you put your application in a container and then use an orchestrator to provide fault tolerance. Automating resilience is a good example of where microservices, containers and dynamic management work particularly well together.

Microservices for margin

Switching to a more modern example, if your monolithic application is running out of memory on your giant cloud instance, then you have to buy a bigger instance, even if you're hardly using any computing power. However, if your memory-intensive function was split out into its own microservice, you could scale that independently and possibly use a more specialised machine type for hosting it. A flexible microservices architecture can give you more hosting options, which generally cuts your costs.

What's the catch?

If this all sounds too good to be true, it is. As with any distributed architecture, microservices are complex to manage. Distributed systems have ways of failing that you've never thought of before. As Leslie Lamport once put it in a 1987 email, 'A distributed system is one in which the failure of a computer you didn't even know existed can render your own computer unusable.'

The dilemma is what to prioritise.

If you want your system to be easy for your developers, you can architect your microservices for that. Your architecture will probably involve a lot of asynchronous external queues (stateful services) to minimise unpredictable data loss and it will be expensive to host and relatively slow to run, but it will be robust and easier to develop on and support. Don't knock that!

However, if you want your system to be hyperscale, hyperfast and cheap, then you'll have to handle more complex distributed failure modes, which we'll talk about in a later chapter. In the short term, it will be more difficult for your developers and they'll have lots to learn.

So, you have an initial decision to make. Do you start with feature velocity and ease or with scale and margin? It's absolutely sensible to start easy and add incremental complexity as you gain familiarity and expertise.

In our experience, people tend to use more than one approach, but if they want to be successful, everyone starts with something relatively straightforward. In the longer term, some services will need to be hyperfast and some just won't.

On top of that, to really get the benefit from microservices they need to be independently deployable, which requires you to pay careful consideration to the boundaries you draw around them, taking into account cohesion, coupling and information hiding. The second edition of Sam Newman's book *Building Microservices* (2015) does an excellent job of exploring this topic in more detail.

Microservice vs monolith

Not all application architectures fully benefit from a cloud native approach. For example, stopping a container fast, which is important to dynamic management, only works if the application inside the container is happy to be stopped quickly. This may not be true if the app is maintaining lots of information about its internal state that needs to be saved when the process terminates. Saving state is slow.

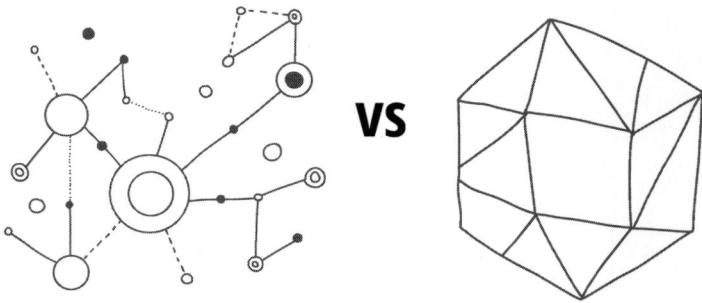

VS

Lots of older applications maintain state because that was how you used to architect things: as big, multipurpose 'monoliths' that were slow to stop and start. You might often still architect that way because it has many benefits; it just happens not to work so well with some aspects of dynamic management.

If you have a monolith there are still advantages to a cloud native approach, but cloud native works optimally for scalability and resilience with a system of small, independent microservices that are quick to stop and start and that communicate with one another via clear interfaces. The scaling and resilience advantages of containers and orchestrators exist whether you've gone for an easy-but-expensive microservice architecture or a hyperscale-and-hyperfast one, or indeed somewhere in between, which is where most people are.

So, there are clear speed, scale, productivity, resilience and cost advantages to using microservices, containers and dynamic management. And they all work even better together. Great! But what about continuous delivery? Is that required too? It is, and we should not forget it!

5 The dream of continuous delivery

In the original CNCF description of cloud native as 'container packaging, dynamic management and a microservices-oriented architecture', there was no mention of continuous integration (CI) or continuous delivery (CD). However, they are both present in every successful cloud native set-up that we've seen – present and vital.

So, this chapter is devoted to the philosophy behind CI/CD. Why would you want it, why is it so hard to achieve and how did people tackle it in the past? Finally, how can it be tackled in a cloud native environment?

Is faster really better?

There's huge variation between comparies in the time it takes for a new product idea to appear in front of users. For some, it's months. For others, it's hours or minutes. Some marketing teams can have a wild thought at 9 am and see it in production that afternoon.

The route followed by the speedier companies to achieve this velocity has not been easy. It has usually taken several years and they've progressed gradually from cloud to continuous delivery to microservices, containers and orchestration. But, before we look into all that, let's step back. What's so good about fast?

The need for speed

It's still not unusual for a tech team to create an 18-month roadmap of planned features. This can be problematic. Good ideas from developers, marketing or even executives can get pushed to the end of the roadmap. By the time these ideas are ready for implementation, the business might have cooled on them and the chance has been missed.

Why is it all so slow? Do all changes take months to implement? Often, no – some might be a few days' work. Are development and operations deliberately obstructive? Usually not – an 18-month roadmap is as frustrating to techies as it is to everyone else. Contrary to popular belief, techies are humans too.

So, what's going on? Actually, quite a few things.

Mega-projects

Mega-projects such as enterprise resource planning (ERP) implementations can take up all the time, brain cycles and positive energy of a tech team for months or years. ERP implementations have few natural break points or early ROI milestones and therefore they have a very long time to value.

Unfortunately, teams involved in mega-projects with a high-risk, single,12-month milestone are unlikely to benefit from a cloud native approach to speed. To go fully cloud native, you need to be able to deploy small, discrete units of value. Sometimes mega-projects are unavoidable, but they are not what this book is about.

Manual tasks and handover

If even small tasks within your tech organisation require manual processes or, even worse, high-friction handovers between multiple parties, then considerable cost and elapsed time are added to every project. For example, the developer who writes the code may have to wait days for their comrade on the ops team to provide a test environment. Multiple handovers can easily delay deployment by weeks. This is an area in which a cloud native strategy could reduce friction by automating or simplifying some of the handover processes.

Monolithic fixes and test cycles

If a bad change could have a catastrophic knock-on effect on your system, then a lot of system-wide and even manual testing may be needed before any change goes live. This problem is further compounded in a complex monolith because it can be difficult to make any change at all. The code is hard to understand, you may not have access to the original coders and you often don't have a comprehensive automated test suite. The risk of making a bad fix is greatly increased.

In this risky environment, it makes sense to batch changes together for testing so you don't need to go through your lengthy test process too often. But waiting on test cycles introduces loads of project delay. Fully automated testing is generally a requirement for fast deployment. However, retrofitting that to a legacy monolith is often impractical.

A microservices-oriented approach is designed to reduce the scope and therefore risk of changes and the length of test cycles. If a service is small and essentially decoupled from other services, then the scope of required testing is reduced and it's far more automatable. You just need to test that the small service itself isn't broken and that any interfaces it exposes are maintained. You can then rely on a fix not breaking your whole system. If every service is small and decoupled that happily limits the damage the occasional, and inevitable, bug can do in production.

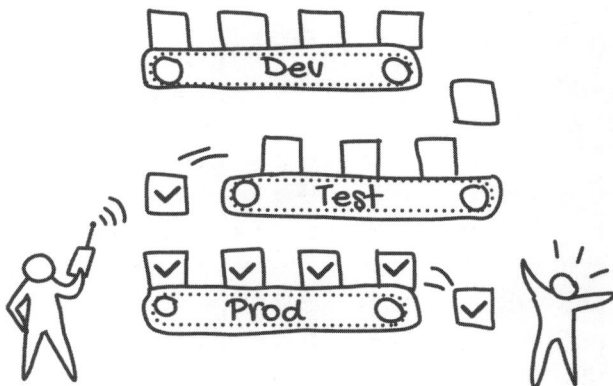

Long provisioning cycles

Imagine an environment in which enterprises buy and maintain their own hardware. If new machinery needs to be bought, housed and installed for a project, this can add months to the delivery date. In the cloud world of cloud native, hardware is hired. It's housed remotely by someone else and bought on demand. Production, test and even development environments can be provisioned and reprovisioned as needed. Infrastructure decisions are de-risked: far less planning is required upfront and months of potential delay can be avoided.

Slowness breeds slowness

There are also problems generated by the slowness itself. The devil makes work for idle hands and developers who are sitting around waiting for sign-off often gold-plate their functions (ie add nice-to-have features that will introduce bugs and require testing but are probably of less value than the agreed functionality).

Is slow so bad?

Why is slow a problem? Again, there are multiple reasons:

- ↳ **Time to value**: If an idea is successful, you've just wasted years of potential revenue and progress.
- ↳ **Demoralisation**: Why bother suggesting ideas that never get implemented?
- ↳ **Missed opportunities**: Every idea has a shelf life. A faster-moving company may step in.
- ↳ **Disappointed users**: In a world of glacial progress, bugs don't get fixed and products con't evolve.
- ↳ **A big gamble**: Finally, if slow also equals large, then you're making a significant gamble on the future a year or two years ahead. For some projects, the odds justify this – but in fast-moving sectors, they often don't.

Any alternative?

In the past, most of the reasons for slow delivery have been about reducing the risk of breaking something that works or of spending lots of money on something that fails. What if experimentation were lower risk? Let's look at continuous delivery. Is it just an unrealistic dream? Or something potentially more useful?

Continuous delivery

We've looked at why development is often slow and concluded that slowness is commercially bad but there may be good reasons for it: usually the mitigation of technical risk.

If small ideas could move from inception to delivery in days or hours, that could be extremely useful. Businesses could innovate safely, trial new ideas and drop them if they didn't work, with no sunk cost. That would reduce commercial risks for a business.

So, what would happen if moving quickly wasn't

technically risky? Businesses – even large ones – would be free to experiment, to take creative gambles and to learn from failure. Users would get products that evolved faster to their (hopefully) surprise and delight. Businesses would be incentivised to make small, incremental product changes with fast return on investment (ROI). Developers call this concept continuous delivery, or CD. The goal of CD is every step in the deployment and test process from dev to production being automated, safe and fast.

CI/CD tools such as Bamboo, CircleCI, Jenkins or TeamCity help with continuous delivery, but they are not all you need. In order for CD to work effectively, you also need tests to complete without manual intervention, ie automated testing. A product that doesn't have enough automated tests gets much less benefit from CD.

Is CD good for everyone?

For a monolith, it can be extremely hard to convert all required testing into automated processes and it may not be worth the effort. We have made the decision before to not change the legacy core very often, live with a slow test cycle and focus our speedy creative efforts elsewhere. Many companies carve off the bits of a monolith that they want to change a lot, turn those into microservices and leave the rest as is.

Sometimes it's OK to 'sweat your assets' like this, ie benefit from a legacy product without investing heavily in new features. We've all worked on successful products that have continued in this mode for more than 20 years and subsidised more experimental new projects. Existing systems such as the recipe for Coca-Cola can work fine without daily updates.

Observe, orient, decide and act (OODA)

To understand some of the philosophy behind fast and iterative development, let's take a look at a guy who, with his famous OODA loop, gets a lot of airtime at tech conferences: US Air Force Colonel John Boyd. Colonel Boyd was a Korean War aerial combat expert who studied dogfights such as those between MiG-15 and F-86 fighter planes.

Boyd asserted that pilots who could observe (O) the situation, orient themselves (O), decide (D) what to do and then act (A) more quickly would win. Basically, victors reacted more quickly in an unpredictable environment. Boyd called this the OODA loop because pilots had to observe, orient, decide and act over and over again throughout a dogfight in order to triumph. The quicker they could go through this loop (the more reactive they were), the more likely they'd win. Boyd's final observation was a very interesting one. He concluded that 'speed of iteration beats quality of iteration'. Another way of putting this is that in an unpredictable environment, you need to take small steps and lots of them as fast as possible – or if you want goals, take a lot of shots at the goal.

Interestingly, Boyd's conclusions match the more modern work of psychologist Professor Richard Wiseman of the UK's University of Hertfordshire. His research shows that individuals can make themselves luckier by maximising their opportunities (ie by trying lots of sensible stuff quickly).

Now act: but what about observing, orienting and deciding?

If we've automated our deployment processes using continuous delivery plus test automation, then we've already covered the act part of OODA. But what about the other parts? They don't seem to be addressed by CD and test automation. Surely we need to observe, orient and decide as quickly as we now deploy, otherwise these steps become the new bottlenecks?

In fact, they often do become the bottlenecks. Most enterprises speed up the act step with CD and test automation first and then address the observe, orient and decide parts at a later stage.

Next: observe and orient automatically

After a team has automated deployment, it's often left with a manual process for determining whether a change was good or bad against a success metric such as conversions or user sign-ups.

It's fine for this metric-checking to be manual to start with. However, for hyperspeed turnaround, some enterprises are automating the process of measuring success. Full automation of the observe and orient steps would require associating a change with a specific deployment, testing its success against your metric(s) and rolling it back if it has a negative impact. At the moment, this level of automation is still mostly a dream, although some enterprises are moving fast towards it.

Finally: decide differently

The goal of hyperfast deployment is that everyone is deploying several times a day. At that point, given our current product and project management methodologies (waterfall or agile), the decisions on what to deploy will become the pinch point.

Judgements on what to deploy tomorrow may depend on the results of what went live yesterday. That's too fast a turnaround even for weekly agile sprints. Given that strategic decisions have now become low risk, some companies are taking a completely different approach: communicating high-level goals, encouraging information exchange and collaboration between different teams (inside and outside of tech), and then letting developers and teams decide what to build and deploy. Communicate, collaborate and then delegate.

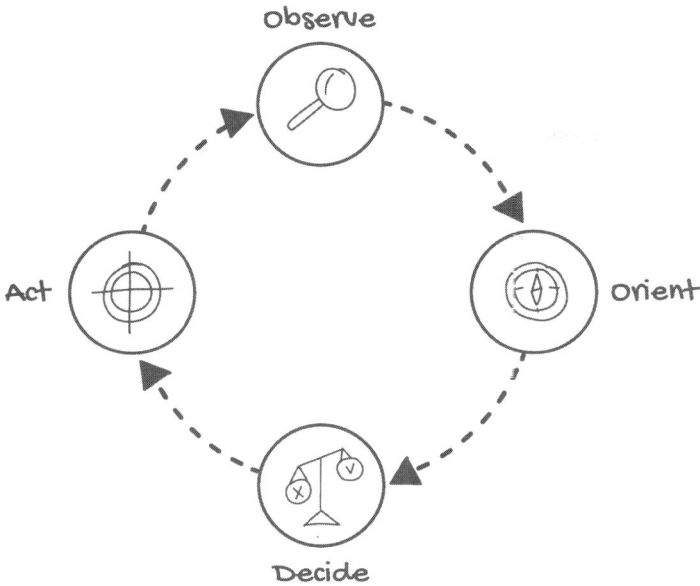

Observe

Orient

Decide

Act

Déjà vu?

What did we do about the speed problem in the past? Many businesses have succeeded without this speed. What have they been doing about this for the past decade or so? Actually, they were painfully aware of the slowness issue and solved it successfully in a very specific, limited but high-value area.

More than 20 years ago, the earliest moves towards multiple daily deployments were made with products called content management systems (CMS). A CMS like WordPress or Joomla! is a tool for allowing multiple people, often designers or copywriters, to make content changes to a website quickly and safely. These deployments can be quite sophisticated and can significantly change the functionality and layout of the site. Ecommerce has exploited the CMS concept well.

CMS principles match those of continuous delivery quite closely:

45

↪ Multiple CMS content deployments are made per day, per person. There's a high rate of change and fast implementation (often within hours) of ideas that come from designers themselves or from marketing or other parts of the business. This is exactly what CD aims to achieve.

↪ The impact of changes is instantly assessed using performance measurement tools (such as Google Analytics) and well-understood techniques such as A/B testing (where you deploy two variants of a change and see which one performs best). This comparative assessment is also CD best practice.

↪ CMS users, eg designers, are embedded within the main business and collaborate constantly with marketeers and other non-techies to make changes. None of this required product managers. If you think that's just natural, remember that 15 years ago those graphic designers were usually in the tech team.

From a technical perspective CMSes work because:

↪ Deployments are low-risk. CMS systems are designed so that deployments apply only to a limited area of the website. A CMS change can't break the whole site. Risk minimisation is also exactly what CD combined with small, discrete microservices is aiming to achieve.

↪ CMS users create and test their own deployments and are responsible for them. They often take changes all the way to production with a fast sign-off process. This kind of personal responsibility is also a key feature of CD.

Can we learn anything from the similarity between the old approach of CMSes and the new tech of CD? CMSes revolutionised e-business by ensuring high-value web content changes (text, HTML and JavaScript) could not break the whole website and could therefore be expedited to production. CMSes allowed enterprises to constantly innovate and update their user-facing content and design without endangering their service or joining the roadmap of doom. This flexibility created new business teams outside of IT devoted to conceptualising, creating and deploying changes quickly. But a CMS only allowed fast evolution in one area: website content. The dream of continuous delivery is to offer this speed and flexibility for every product.

Cloud native and the speed of the internet

To achieve speed, cloud native strategies use continuous delivery, automated testing, microservices or FaaS, container-isation and deployment via orchestrators. Fortunately, not all of these are required at once. You can build up gradually. Sufficient automated testing, however, is probably the first step.

Enterprises may feel they're not ready for CD, but if they have a CMS, they've already done CD for one high-value product. They just did it so long ago they now take it for granted.

As CMSes show, the effect of faster deployments on any business is radical. It extends far beyond the IT department. The reason that media or retail websites are able to update their content multiple times a day is because they have new, non-IT departments that decide on, deliver and deploy that content.

If every web content change still passed through IT using a waterfall or even agile methodology, then even if the updates were being applied using a CMS, you would not see the web content rates of change you currently do.

The lesson from the past is that companies that fully exploit continuous delivery will probably move the people who develop and deploy changes closer to those with a vision for the business and products, and they'll just deploy stuff together without much day-to-day IT involvement.

No business has yet to grow out of the concept of a CMS, and once they have it, we suspect no business will grow out of continuous delivery. For most companies, it's the second step after automated testing, and the first cloud native strategy to pursue.

On that note, we've discussed a lot of what you can potentially do with a cloud native approach but no one does all of it, at least not at once. In the next chapter we'll look at where you can begin.

6 Where to start: the mythical blank slate

A company of any size might start a project that appears to be an architectural blank slate. Hooray! Developers love blank slates. It's a chance to do everything properly, not like those cowboys last time. A blank-slate project is common for a start-up, but a large enterprise can also be in this position. However:

↳ even a start-up with no existing codebase still has legacy

↳ the existing knowledge and experience within your team is valuable, whether or not it includes microservices, FaaS, containers or orchestrators

↳ there may be existing third-party products or open-source code that could really help your project but which may not be cloud native

↳ you may possess useful internal code, tools or processes from other projects that don't fit the cloud native model.

Legacy is not always a bad thing. It's the abundance and reuse of our legacy that allows the software industry to move so quickly. For example, Linux is a codebase that demonstrates some of the common pros and cons of legacy (eg it's a decent OS and widely used but it's bloated, insecure and hardly anyone can support it). Currently, the Linux pros outweigh the cons.

Using your valuable legacy might help you start faster but push you away from a cloud native approach. So what do you do?

What's your problem?

Consider the problems that cloud native is designed to solve: fast and iterative delivery, scale and margin. Are any of these actually your most pressing problem? Right now they might not be. Cloud native requires an investment in time and effort and that effort won't pay off if neither speed (feature velocity), scale or margin are your prime concern.

Thought experiment one: repackaging a monolith

Imagine you're an enterprise with an existing monolithic product that with some minor tweaks and repositioning could be suited to a completely new market. Your immediate problem is not iterative delivery (you can tweak your existing product fairly easily). Scale is not yet an issue and neither is margin (because you don't yet know if the product will succeed). Your goal is to get a usable product live as quickly and cheaply as possible to assess interest.

Alternatively, you may be a start-up who could rapidly produce a proof of concept to test your market using a monolithic framework such as Ruby on Rails with which your team is already familiar.

So, you potentially have two options:

↳ Develop a new cloud native product from scratch using a microservices architecture.
↳ Rapidly create a monolith minimum viable product (MVP), launch the new product on the cloud and measure interest.

In this case, the most low-risk initial strategy might be option two, even if it's less fashionable and cloud native-y. If the product is successful, then you can reassess. If it fails, at least it did so quickly and you aren't too emotionally attached to it.

Thought experiment two: it worked – now scale!

Imagine you chose to build the MVP monolith in thought experiment one and you rapidly discovered that there's a huge market for your new product. Your problem now is that the monolith won't scale to support your potential customer base.

What should you do next?

As a result of the very successful MVP strategy, even though it won't scale, you've learned a lot. You understand the market better and know it's large enough to be worth making some investment. You may now decide that your next problem is scale. You could choose to implement a new version of your product using a scalable microservices approach – or you may not just yet. There are always good arguments either way and more than one way to scale. Have the discussions and make a reasoned decision. Ultimately, having to move from a monolith to a cloud native architecture is not the end of the world, as we'll hear next.

The monolithic legacy

However you arrive at it, a monolithic application is often your actual starting point for a cloud native strategy. Why not just throw it out and start again?

1.    2. 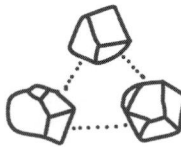   3.

What if the spaghetti is your secret sauce?

It's hard to successfully re-implement legacy products. They always contain more high-value features than is immediately apparent. The value may lie in years of workarounds for obscure field issues (we've been there). Or maybe the hidden value is in undocumented behaviours that are now taken for granted and relied upon by users (we've been there too).

Underestimated, evolved value increases the cost and pain of replacing older legacy systems, but it is real value and you don't want to lose it. If you have an evolved, legacy monolith, converting it to microservices is not easy or safe. However, it might be the correct next step.

So, what are people doing? How do they accomplish the move from monolith to microservices?

Can a monolith benefit from cloud native?

There are lots of potential approaches to moving a legacy monolith to the cloud. You can even use simpler approaches as stepping stones to more involved approaches. Fundamentally, you don't have to leap to a microservice architecture in one bound. An incremental approach is perfectly reasonable:

> ↳ The simplest approach is often to wrap an existing monolith in a container and just put it on a cloud

52

VM (either orchestrated or not). This step provides benefits in terms of ease of management of the containerised application image and more streamlined testing and deployment. Potentially, there are also security advantages in immutable container image deployments.

↳ Second, you might take an 'API-first' architectural approach, splitting the monolithic application into a stateless and scalable front end and a stateful (fairly monolithic) back end with a clear API on the back end. Being stateless, the front end becomes easier to scale. This step improves scalability and resilience, and potentially margin via orchestration.

↳ Third, you could break up the stateful and monolithic back end into increasingly smaller components, some of which are stateless. You could split out the API at this point into its own service: this further improves scale, resilience and margin. You might also start leveraging useful third-party services such as databases (DBaaS) or managed queues (QaaS).

Businesses that choose to go cloud native often iteratively break up an existing monolithic architecture into smaller and smaller chunks, starting at the front and working backwards, integrating third-party commodity services such as DBaaS as they go. With regular deployment to live, this may be a safer way to re-architect a monolith: inevitably, you'll occasionally still accidentally lose important features, but at least you'll find out about that sooner when it's relatively easier to resolve.

You can see that even a monolith can have an evolutionary strategy for benefiting from a microservice-oriented, containerised and orchestrated approach, without the kind of big-bang rewrite that gives everyone nightmares and often critically undervalues what you already have.

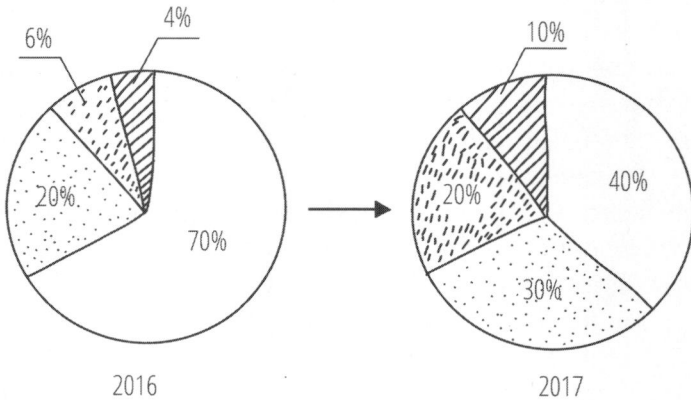

2016 → 2017

Example cloud native strategies

There are lots of different cloud native approaches. You can:

- ↳ start with CI and then add containerisation
- ↳ start with containerisation and then add CI
- ↳ start with microservices and add CI
- ↳ start by breaking up the monolith
- ↳ start with microservices from a clean slate (as far as that exists).

Many enterprises do several of these things at once in different parts of the organisation and then tie them together – or don't.

Is only one of these approaches correct? We take the pragmatic view. From what we've seen, for software 'the proof of the pudding is in the eating'. Software is not moral philosophy. The ultimate value of cloud native should not be intrinsic ('it's on trend' or 'it's more correct'). It should be extrinsic ('it works for us and our clients').

If containers, microservices and orchestration might be useful to you, then try them out iteratively and in the smallest, safest and highest value order for you. If they help, do more. If they don't, do something else.

Things will go wrong; try not to beat yourself up about it. Think about what you learned and attempt something different. No one can foresee the future. A handy alternative is to get there sooner.

In this chapter, we've talked a lot about strategies for moving from monolith to microservices. Surely just starting with microservices is easier? Inevitably, the answer is yes and no. It has different challenges. In the next chapter, we're going to let out our inner pessimists and talk about why distributed systems are so hard. Maybe they obey Conway's law, which states that organisations tend to design systems that copy their communication structures, but they most definitely obey Murphy's law: what can go wrong, will go wrong.

But does that matter?

7 Distributed systems are hard

Nowadays, the industry spends much of its time singing the praises of a cloud native (containerised and microservice-ish) architecture. However, some companies still run monoliths, while some others, such as Segment, broke their monolith into microservices and then, a few years later, went back to a monolithic architecture. Why? It's not merely because those companies are full of renegades bucking the trend. It's because distributed systems are real y hard and often unnecessarily expensive. As software engineer Alexandra Noonan put it at QCon London in 2020, 'If microservices are implemented incorrectly or used as a Band-Aid without addressing some of the root flaws in your system, you'll be unable to do new product development because you're drowning in the complexity.'

Nonetheless, a distributed model is the only way to get hyperscale, truly resilient and fast-responding systems, so you may have to get your head around it.

In this chapter, we'll look at some of the ways in which distributed systems can trip you up and some of the ways in which people are handling those obstacles.

Anything that can go wrong, will go wrong

At scale, things change. The more instances of anything you have, the higher the likelihood that one or more of them will break – and probably at the same time.

Services will fall over before they've received your message, while they're processing your message or after they've processed it but before they've told you they have. The network will lose packets, disks will fail, virtual machines will unexpectedly terminate.

There are things a monolithic architecture guarantees that are no longer true when we've distributed our system. Components (now services) no longer start and stop together in a predictable order. Services may unexpectedly restart, changing their state or their version. The result is that no service can make assumptions about another – the system cannot rely on one-to-one communication.

A lot of the traditional mechanisms for recovering from failure may make things worse in a distributed environment. Brute force retries may flood your network; restores from backups are no longer straightforward. There are design patterns for addressing all of these issues but they require thought and testing.

If there were no errors, distributed systems would be pretty easy. That can lull optimists into a false sense of security. Distributed systems must be designed to be resilient by accepting that 'every possible error' is just business as usual.

What we have here is a failure to communicate

There are traditionally two high-level approaches to application message passing in unreliable (ie distributed) systems:

↳ **Reliable but slow**: Keep a saved copy of every message until you've had confirmation that the next process in the chain has taken full responsibility for it.

↳ **Unreliable but fast**: Send multiple copies of messages to potentially multiple recipients and tolerate message loss and duplication.

The reliable and unreliable application-level communications we're talking about here are not the same as network reliability – eg transmission control protocol (TCP) versus user datagram protocol (UDP). Imagine two stateless services that send messages to one another directly over TCP. Even though TCP is a reliable network protocol, this isn't reliable application-level comms. Either service could fall over and lose a message it had successfully received but not yet processed because stateless services don't securely save the data they're handling.

You could make this set-up application-level-reliable by putting stateful queues between the services to save each message until it had been completely processed. The downside to this is that it would be slower, but you might be happy to live with that if it made life simpler, particularly if you used a managed stateful queue service so you didn't have to worry about the scale and resilience of that.

The reliable approach is predictable but involves delay (latency) and work: lots of confirmation messages and resiliently saving data (statefulness) until you've had sign-off from the next service in the chain that it has taken responsibility for each message.

A reliable approach doesn't guarantee rapid delivery but it does guarantee all messages will be delivered eventually, at least once. In an environment where every message is critical and no loss can be tolerated (for example, credit card transactions), this is a good approach. Amazon Simple Queue Service (Amazon's managed queue service) is one example of a stateful service that can be used in a reliable way.

The second, unreliable, approach involves sending multiple messages and crossing your fingers. It's faster end to end but it means services have to expect duplicates and out-of-order messages, and some messages will go missing. Unreliable service-to-service communication might be used when messages are time sensitive (ie if they're not acted on quickly, it's not worth acting on them, like video frames) or when later data just overwrites earlier data (like the current price of a flight). For very large-scale distributed systems, unreliable messaging may be used because it's faster, with less overhead. However, microservices then need to be designed to cope with message loss and duplication – and forget about order.

Within each approach there are a lot of variants (guaranteed and non-guaranteed order, for example, in reliable comms), all of which have different trade-offs in terms of speed, complexity and failure rate. Some systems may use multiple approaches depending on the type of message being transmitted or even the current load on the system.

This stuff is hard to get right, especially if you have a lot of services all behaving differently. The behaviour of a service needs to be explicitly defined in its API and it often makes sense to define constraints or recommended communication behaviours for the services in your system to get some degree of consistency.

What time is it?

There's no such thing as common time – a global clock – in a distributed system. For example, in a group chat there's usually no guaranteed order in which one person's comments and those sent by their friends in Australia, Colombia and Japan will appear. There isn't even any guarantee they're all seeing the same timeline, although one ordering will generally win out if they sit around long enough without saying anything new.

Fundamentally, in a distributed system, every machine has its own clock and the system as a whole doesn't have one correct time. Machine clocks may get synchronised a lot, but even then, transmission times for the synchronous messages will vary and physical clocks run at different rates, so everything gets out of sync again pretty much immediately.

On a single machine, one clock can provide a common time for all threads and processes. In a distributed system, this is just not physically possible.

In our new world, then, clock time no longer provides an incontrovertible definition of order. The monolithic concept of 'what time is it?' does not exist in a microservice world, and designs should not rely on it for inter-service messages.

The truth is out there

In a distributed system, there's no global shared memory and therefore no single version of the truth. Data will be scattered across physical machines. In addition, any given piece of data is more likely to be in the relatively slow and inaccessible transit between machines than would be the case in a monolith. Decisions therefore need to be based on current, local information.

This means that answers will not always be consistent in different parts of the system. In theory, they should eventually become consistent as information disseminates across the system, but if the data is constantly changing, we may never reach a completely consistent state short of turning off all the new inputs and waiting. Services therefore have to handle the fact that they may get 'old' or inconsistent information in response to their questions.

Talk fast!

In a monolithic application, most of the important communications happen within a single process, between one component and another. Communications inside processes are very quick, so lots of internal messages being passed around is not a problem. However, once you split your monolithic components out into separate services, often running on different machines, things get trickier.

To give you some context:

↳ In the best case, it takes about 100 times longer to send a message from one machine to another than it does to just pass a message internally from one component to another.

↳ Many services use text-based RESTful messages to communicate. RESTful messages are cross platform and easy to use, read and debug, but slow to transmit and receive. In contrast, remote procedure call (RPC) messages paired with binary message protocols are not human readable and are therefore harder to debug and use, but are much faster to transmit and receive. It might be 20 times faster to send a message via an RPC method, of which a popular example is gRPC, than it is to send a RESTful message.

There's also a plethora of other options for inter-service communication, including GraphQL, message brokers such as Kafka and other binary formats such as Simple Binary Encoding, Cap'n Proto and FlatBuffers. Each of these has strengths and weaknesses and none is perfect in every situation. And regardless of which one you choose, inter-service communication still incurs overhead. The upshot of all of this in a distributed environment is that you have two basic options.

- ↳ **Send fewer messages**: You might choose to send fewer and larger messages between distributed microservices than you would send between components in a monolith because every message introduces delays (aka latency).
- ↳ **Consider sending messages more efficiently**: For what you do send, you can help your system run faster by using RPC rather than REST for transmitting messages. Or even just go UDP and handle the unreliability. That will have trade-offs, though, in terms of developer productivity.

Testing to destruction

If your system can change at sub-second speeds, which is the aim of a dynamically managed, distributed architecture, then you need to be aware of issues at that speed. Many traditional logging tools are not designed to track that responsively. You need to make sure you use one that is.

The only way to know if your distributed system works and will recover from unpredictable errors is to continually engineer those errors and continually repair your system. Netflix pioneered the use of chaos testing (known as fault injection testing in academic literature) in a commercial setting using their Chaos Monkey to randomly pull cables and crash instances. Over time, they've expanded this into a whole suite of open-source tools referred to as the Simian Army. Likewise, Facebook developed Project Storm to test the resistance of its infrastructures to extreme events. Other options here include ChaosMachine, which does chaos engineering at the application level in the Java virtual machine (JVM); Proofdock's Chaos Engineering Platform, which focuses on Azure; and Gremlin's 'failure as a service' product.

Any test tool needs to test your system for resilience and integrity and, just as importantly, test your logging and observability to make sure that if an error occurs you can diagnose and fix it retrospectively – ie after you have brought your system back online.

This all sounds difficult. Do I have to?

Creating a distributed, scalable, resilient system is extremely tough, particularly for stateful services. Now is the time to decide whether you need it, or at least need it immediately. Can your customers live with slower responses or lower scale for a while? That would make your life easier because you could design a smaller, slower, simpler system first and only add more complexity as you build expertise.

Cloud providers such as AWS, Google and Azure are constantly improving offerings that could do increasingly large parts of this hard stuff for you, particularly resilient statefulness (managed queues and databases). These services can seem costly but building and maintaining complex distributed services is expensive too.

Any framework that constrains you but handles some of this complexity is well worth considering. Service meshes such as Istio, Linkerd or Cilium are worth considering. A service mesh will typically give you increased observability of the traffic in the cluster and sophisticated routing between microservices, and can also improve both resiliency and security. However, they add their own complexity and can be CPU intensive, which is a sustainability issue.

The key takeaway is: don't underestimate how hard building a properly resilient and highly scalable service is. In summary:

↳ Decide whether you really need it all yet. You probably don't.

↳ Educate everyone thoroughly.

↳ Introduce useful constraints.

↳ Start simple; use tools and services wherever possible.

↳ Do everything gradually.

↳ Expect setbacks as well as successes.

8 The sustainability attitude

Until recently, the global emissions from data centres had grown only modestly year on year. However, since the advent of ChatGPT and the other LLMs, electricity use by DCs has risen significantly, putting the climate commitments of major cloud providers in peril.

The good news is that building green or sustainable AI can be done and requires the same approach as creating a modern cloud native system. For more about that, read the sustainability chapter in *Building Green Software*, Anne's book on the subject (2024).

Aside from ensuring we still have a planet to live on, building sustainable software has a lot of more immediately tangible business benefits, not the least of which is that it can save you money. It can also help your environmental, social and governance (ESG) score, which is something firms, at least in Europe, are increasingly using as part of vendor selection criteria. As an industry, we all need to be paying attention, and fortunately, as efforts such as the 'Principles of Green Software Engineering' show, we are starting to.

It has to be said, though, that no enterprise we have ever come across went cloud native because they wanted to be more green. They should have, however, and in the future we predict that's exactly what they'll do. The good news is that a cloud native approach has the ability to be more efficient and therefore sustainable, which is mostly down to the public cloud's vast scale.

In the short term, climate change will be the single most irrefutable argument for adopting a cloud native architecture. The tech equivalent of hugging trees will be to hug Lambda instances, but why on Planet A do we think that?

To efficiency and beyond

According to the Linux Foundation's Green Software Foundation, building sustainable, aka green, software systems comes down to maximising three things:

- ↳ **Software efficiency**: Fewer CPU cycles means less electricity used, which means less carbon emitted to generate that electricity.
- ↳ **Hosting efficiency**: Hosting a system on fewer machines uses less CPU/electricity and requires less embodied carbon, which is the carbon emitted as part of the manufacture of any hardware.
- ↳ **Carbon awareness**: Not all electricity is equal. If you can target computation at times when low-carbon power like solar or wind is available, carbon emissions are reduced by a huge amount. This piece of the energy transition puzzle is vital and often overlooked.

Quite by chance, the cloud handles all three of these vastly better than on-premises data centres.

The green revolution

Actually, the fact that the cloud is greener than on-premises data centres did not happen by chance. We don't know for sure, but maybe it's because Jeff Bezos is a secret social justice warrior.

Not convinced? If you find that hard to swallow, there's another explanation. Sustainability is directly correlated with cost cutting for hypercloud providers. Even if it has traditionally never been a marketing feature, it's a major commercial benefit to AWS, Google and Azure to be green.

How green? According to AWS's chief evangelist Jeff Barr, 'On average, AWS customers use 77 per cent fewer servers, 84 per cent less power, and utilise a 28 per cent cleaner power mix, for a total reduction in carbon emissions of 88 per cent from using the AWS Cloud instead of operating their own data centres.'

Speaking on the Container Solutions podcast *Hacking the Org*, former AWS VP of sustainability architecture Adrian Cockcroft said that this was down to 'a combination of much higher utilisation, more efficient machines end to end, and then all of the cloud vendors are building large wind farms, solar farms and battery farms. So, for literally all the cloud vendors in Europe and the US right now, you're pretty much at zero scope two carbon, which is the carbon burnt by the machines. Most of the carbon that needs to be eliminated right now is in Asia.'

But while an 88 per cent reduction just for moving to the cloud sounds like an amazing win, we should note that a move to the cloud is only *potentially* more carbon efficient and aware. It depends on the choice of regions, server density, managed services and spot instances. In other words the cloud *can* be a lot more sustainable than on-prem but, unfortunately, that's not baked in. Like so many things in life, it's what you do with the cloud that matters.

Location, location, location

If you lift and shift legacy systems into the cloud and put them on dedicated VMs or even bare metal machines, then you won't be that much greener than if you had left them where they were. However, your green credentials may still be better because all the hypercloud providers have committed to buying the lowest carbon electricity they can get their hands on. They have a lot of clout to make that happen, and they appear to be delivering. This should mean that less carbon-intensive power will be running all cloud compute. Unfortunately, though, that doesn't solve everything. There are still problems.

There's an excellent chance that in any particular location, the public cloud will have the cleanest power going. Nevertheless, region matters. You might still get greener electricity by operating an on-prem data centre (DC) somewhere with plenty of zero-carbon energy, like Iceland, with its geothermal resources, or Greenland, with its water power. It's better to avoid or minimise your use of regions with too much dirty power, like the coal-fuelled state of Virginia (home of EC1!) or, as Adrian Cockcroft pointed out, more or less anywhere in Asia.

Nonetheless, the cloud has a wide range of moderately or very clean regions to choose from and those greener options are growing. For that reason, and because it is often more difficult than you might imagine to move systems between regions, we recommend that you look at sustainability information before choosing a region, and choose a cloud provider who makes this easy.

However, relatively clean energy and the ability to choose your location are not the cloud's only green advantages.

Scale pays

Efficiency saves money. It reduces data centre hardware and space requirements and cuts electricity bills. But the trouble is that creating an efficient software system costs a great deal of cash upfront. It's difficult and it's time and staff intensive. You'll also face a lot of pushback from your developers, most of whom hate writing software in efficient but tricky languages such as Rust or C because it's comparatively slow and painstaking. They'd rather use Python, which is unfortunate because, at least according to research from Rui Pereira et al (2017), it's one of the least efficient languages by quite some way.

More complexity also means more support and maintenance costs; your marketing team will rebel at your slow feature releases; and, to ice the cake, those C or Rust developers cost a fortune.

The good news is, while it's unlikely to ever beat C or Rust here, Java is, perhaps surprisingly, quite efficient. In truth, though, if your company isn't big, the ops savings from efficiency often aren't worth the hassle, if they even materialise at all after you factor in the additional development, opportunity and maintenance costs. Super-efficiency frequently only pays off once you have achieved super-scale and your electricity bills start looking like Bill Gates's bank balance. Enterprises don't always achieve that scale, but you know who does? The hyperscale cloud providers. The clue is in the name.

Google, Microsoft and AWS hire the very best developers so you don't have to. These specialist developers can then use their huge, high-maintenance brains to produce whizzy orchestrators to tightly pack VMs or containers onto physical servers and achieve maximal hardware efficiency. They can also optimise the cloud's managed services such as DBaaS or code platforms such as Firecracker (which underlies AWS's Lambda service). These smart services are not only highly efficient but offer things such as autoscaling, which provides system resilience with fewer machines.

It's only worth the hyperclouds putting in the Herculean effort to develop that stuff because millions of people use their services. As we said, scale matters when it comes to efficiency. Fundamentally, managed services, of which serverless is the most extreme example, are more efficient and therefore greener than anything you can build or operate yourself. In our opinion, that's one of the most important and least appreciated features of a cloud native approach.

Scale and commoditisation, however, are not entirely without their issues. If something is cheap and provides a useful service, you'll use more of it – aka the Jevons paradox, which says that as something increases in efficiency, demand will *increase* rather than decrease. It's your responsibility to ensure that what you do with that benefits society.

Shift and shape

Efficient systems are not the only thing you get from the cloud. Sometimes carbon emissions are all about when and where you perform tasks. For sustainability, latency-insensitive workloads are as useful as efficient systems. Why?

There are two things we know about renewable power:

↳ It's super cheap when it's available.
↳ It isn't always on tap in a particular locality.

The safest and more efficient choice is for electricity to be used as close in space and time as possible to where it was generated. Electricity doesn't like to travel that far through a grid. The most obvious reason for that is that too much of it gets lost through resistance, but having too much electricity slopping around for too long is also dangerous because it risks blown-out connections. Grids often handle that by dumping power as part of their normal grid-balancing operations. What a waste! The upshot of this is that, at some times and places, electricity is expensive and at others it's cheap: you might even be paid to use it rather than the grid having to dump it.

Ideally, at times when electricity is dirty and expensive, you wouldn't use it at all. If you have to, you want to use it efficiently. When it's cheap, though, any efficiency savings are unlikely to be worthwhile. That will change in future when the new bottleneck becomes hardware, but we have a few years before that happens, and by then the world might come up with a better way to extend hardware lifespans to solve the problem.

The reality of renewable power is that it doesn't play nicely with heavyweight, always-on services like legacy monoliths sitting in on-prem DCs. However, it works extremely well with systems that can delay work until the sun comes up or the wind starts blowing. This is called demand shifting, and the best commodity service to help you do it already exists in the cloud. It's called a spot instance or, over at Google, preemptible instances.

For what is usually an approximately 90 per cent cost discount to the user, spot instances give a cloud provider the scope to shift a job in both time and location of execution. At the moment, that usually improves their hardware utilisation (better server density through tight job packing onto servers), but Google is already using the technique to take advantage of the availability of greener electricity.

In the final analysis, writing green software is often more difficult and expensive than building old-school, always-on monoliths. That makes it an excellent candidate for getting someone else to do it for you. Ideally, that would be a specialist who can deploy their code at the scale required for the additional development cost to pay off. Fortunately, the scale and specialist services of the cloud, coupled with the cloud providers' selfish motivation to cut their own energy costs, means a cloud native approach should be a greener one.

9 Insights from case studies

Over the last decade we have conducted multiple interviews with different businesses using a cloud native approach at the heart of their work, in some cases revisiting them as markets and technology have evolved. In this chapter we'll share some of the useful findings and insights from these.

Early adopter case studies are usually only moderately useful. Successful businesses are unique with their own goals and risk profiles, and the very early adopters of cloud native had a different attitude to risk than those starting out or restructuring now. However, these later adopters are more realistic role models for the average enterprise than Google or Netflix.

Method

In 2017 and 2018, we conducted multiple interviews with some of the earliest, real-world enterprise practitioners of the cloud native philosophy. The available tools and services have evolved somewhat since then, but their experiences of taking their first steps in that environment and the architectural decisions they made remain fascinating and equally relevant today.

What we wanted from the original 2017/2018 interviews was to understand:

↪ what was their aim?

↪ what issues and roadblocks did they hit?

↪ did they get what they wanted?

The case studies give us a general idea of what industry pioneers did, how difficult it was and whether the path became any easier over time. Each covers the point at which the companies began to become successful with a cloud native approach, which wasn't always at their first attempt. At the end of each case study, we revisit them to hear about what they've learned in the years since. We also spoke to cinch, arguably one of the UK's most successful start-ups, and a company that has pursued a 'serverless first' approach, pivoting to AWS Lambda from Kubernetes.

Case study 1: Financial Times (2017)

Based in London, in 2017 the *Financial Times* had an average worldwide daily readership of 2.2 million. Its paid circulation, including both print and digital, was 856,000. Three quarters of its subscribers were digital.

The *FT* was a pioneer of content paywalls and the first mainstream UK newspaper to report earning more from digital subscriptions than print sales. It's also unusual in earning more from content than from advertising.

Starting in 2014, the *FT* gradually adopted microservices, continuous delivery, containers and orchestrators. Like Skyscanner (which we'll talk about next), its original motivation was to be able to move faster and respond more quickly to changes in the marketplace.

As Sarah Wells, the high-profile tech lead of the content platform, pointed out: 'Our goal of becoming a techno-logically agile company was a major success – the teams moved from provisioning a server taking 120 days to only 15 minutes.' In the process, according to senior project manager Victoria Morgan-Smith, 'The teams were completely liberated.' So, how did they achieve all this? Broadly speaking, they made incremental but constant improvements.

The *FT* moved an increasing share of its infrastructure into the cloud (IaaS). In 2011, it started with its own virtualised infrastructure but then adopted AWS as Amazon solved issues with funding, monitoring, networking and OS choice. As Sarah Wells described it, 'Custom infrastructure was not a business differentiator for us.' In 2017, it had set a target of moving to 100 per cent cloud infrastructure and wherever possible used off-the-shelf, cloud-based services such as databases as a service (including AWS Aurora) and queues as a service. Again this is because operating this functionality in-house was 'not a differentiator' for the company.

Within the *FT* as a whole, there was a strong inclination to move to a microservices-oriented architecture, but in different parts of the company teams took different approaches. The *FT* had three big programmes of work where it implemented a new system as a set of microservices. One of those (subscription services) incrementally migrated a monolithic server to a microservice architecture by slowly carving off key components. However, the remaining two projects (the new content platform and the new website) essentially each built a duplicate of their respective monoliths right from the start using microservices. Interestingly, both of those approaches worked successfully for the *FT*, suggesting that there's no one correct way to do a monolith-to-microservices migration.

After nearly three years, the content platform had moved from a monolith to having around 150 microservices, each of which broadly 'does one thing'. However, the teams had not followed the popular 'Conway's law' approach, where one or more microservices represent the responsibilities of each team (many services to one team). Instead, multiple teams supported each microservice (many to many). This helped to maximise parallelism, but was mostly done because teams worked end to end on the delivery of features (such as 'publish videos') and these features usually spanned multiple microservices. Teams were then monitored for deployment conflicts. If clashes regularly occurred, then the service in contention was split further.

Across the *FT*, in Wells' words, 'Infrastructure as code was necessary for microservices', and a strong culture of automation and CD emerged. According to Wells, 'There is a fair amount of diversity within the *FT*, with some teams running a home-grown continuous delivery system based on Puppet while others wrap and deploy their services in Docker containers on the container-friendly Linux operating system CoreOS, with yet others deploying to Heroku.'

Basically, in 2017 there was:

↳ a home-grown, Puppet-based platform, hosted on AWS without containers
↳ a Heroku-hosted PaaS
↳ a Docker container-based environment using CoreOS, hosted on AWS.

All of these environments worked well: each was evolving and was chosen by the relevant tech team to meet their own needs at the time. Again, the *FT*'s experience suggests there's more than one way to successfully implement an architectural vision that's microservice oriented and runs in a cloud-based environment with continuous delivery.

Finally, the *FT*'s content platform team found that containers were the gateway to orchestration. By 2017, the content folk had been orchestrating their Docker-containerised processes in production for several years with the original motivation being server density, with more efficient resource utilisation. By using large AWS instances to host multiple containerised processes, controlled with an orchestrator, they reduced their hosting costs by around 75 per cent. As very early users of orchestration, they created their own orchestrator from several open-source tools, but by 2017 were evaluating the latest off-the-shelf products, in particular Kubernetes.

So, what unexpected results came out of this cloud native evolution? The *FT* anticipated the shift to faster deployments would increase risk. In fact, it moved from a 20 per cent deployment rollback rate to approximately 0.1 per cent, ie a two-orders-of-magnitude reduction in error rate. The *FT* ascribed this to the ability to release small changes more often with microservices. It invested heavily in monitoring and A/B testing, again building its own tools for the latter, and replaced traditional pre-deployment acceptance tests with automated monitoring in production of key functionality.

How did it handle the complexity of distributed systems? It chose to make heavy use of asynchronous queues as a service, which simplified its distributed architecture by limiting the knock-on effects of a single microservice outage (although this did increase system latency, a trade-off it accepted). It also limited the use of chained synchronous calls to avoid cascading failures, when one failed service holds up a whole chain of services waiting on outstanding synchronous requests. It contemplated exit rules to combat issues around the order of microservice instantiation, ie allowing the orchestrator to exit and then automatically restart microservices if prerequisite services were not yet available (by which point their prerequisite service should hopefully have appeared). Basically, it was difficult but the *FT* learned and improved along the way.

According to Victoria Morgan-Smith, 'Our goal throughout was to de-risk experimentation', but that involved 'training, tools and trust'. The *FT* heavily invested in internal on-the-job training with an explicit remit for their DevOps teams to disseminate the new operational knowledge to other developers and operations teams. It learned that its teams could be trusted to make good judgements if they were informed, given responsibility and had the right tools. For example, initially its IaaS bills were very high, but once developers were given training, access to billing tools and guidance on budgets, the bills reduced.

In common with many other early adopters, the *FT* experimented, built in-house and was prepared to accept a level of uncertainty and risk. Sometimes the tech teams needed to reassess as the world changed, as with their move from private to public cloud, but they were persistent and trusted to make the occasional readjustment in a rapidly changing environment. Trust was a key factor in their progress.

The Financial Times revisited (2023)

Dewi Rees and Sarah Wells, current and former technical directors for engineering enablement at the Financial Times, *write:*

Since 2017, the *Financial Times* has increased subscriber numbers across print and digital to 1.25 million; 90 per cent of its subscribers are now digital.

The *FT* has continued to see benefits from adopting a cloud native approach. In 2021, there were around 100 code deployments every working day, several hundred times as many as in the days of monolithic architectures.

We continued our move to the cloud, decommissioning our last data centre late in 2020. This saved us a fair bit of money but also let us go beyond running applications in a VM. Now, every system is built somewhere that offers to do at least some of the work for us and teams make use of the tools that cloud providers offer: managed databases, functions as a service, managed queues.

The FT still uses a microservice architecture and there are also still a number of different deployment approaches. Generally, the FT has moved away from home-grown options as the microservices ecosystem has matured. So, for example, the CoreOS-based container orchestrator that the content platform team had built was replaced first with Kubernetes and then with EKS, AWS's managed Kubernetes platform.

This change provided a solution to the issues around the order of microservice instantiation: the team configured liveness and readiness probes and Kubernetes handled things; they also achieved a better utilisation of the underlying computational resources via the configuration of node affinities and taints.

Handing off the day-to-day running of infrastructure has been a theme, with the adoption of SaaS solutions, heavy use of serverless such as AWS Lambda and continued use of Heroku alongside other PaaS options such as Platform.sh.

Conway's law did catch up with us a bit. The FT is divided into groups of five to ten teams that own large subsystems made up of many microservices. Now, there is much more of an alignment between services and teams, with each service owned by a single team. As an example, the content programme within the core group has split the domain, with one team focusing on content and another on metadata.

This strong ownership is tracked in the FT's Biz Ops tool, an internal system that has allowed us to keep track of a graph of information about our services. This includes teams, systems, repositories, AWS resources, incidents – any information that provides value can be added into the graph.

Biz Ops also sits at the centre of a set of tools that provide insight into our full software estate and helps the *FT* to manage it. For example, is the support documentation complete? Are there security warnings that need to be responded to?

Strong ownership is important because at the *FT* each team handles its own deployments to production and is responsible for that system running in production: 'You build it, you run it.' There's still a first-level operations team that triages problems and will run through troubleshooting guides, and there's support at a platform level when things go wrong there. There aren't too many out-of-hours callouts to teams and so a best endeavours approach has been OK, as opposed to a strict rota for each set of systems. People who are willing to take part in out-of-hours support are listed in a spreadsheet and the first-line team will call them round-robin until they find someone available and able to help, keeping track so that it's not always the same people being called.

Autonomous teams choosing the right tools for their needs has left the *FT* with a high level of complexity in the software estate. There are several thousand services, written in three main programming languages (Node.js, Go and Python) and with high variation in the build and deployment tooling. This is a challenge both for governance and for cost control. Over the past few years, there has been more focus on standardisation where things are not a differentiator, and we invested heavily in being able to track cost and compliance and notify teams when something looks like it needs to be addressed.

In 2021, we set up an engineering enablement group, bringing together every team that had engineers as customers, and focused on developer productivity. This group is aiming to 'pave the road', building solutions for common problems to avoid duplication of effort. There has been a focus on self-service solutions to enable teams to keep moving fast: the role of this group is to act as a platform for enabling teams (in the *Team Topologies* sense [see case study 4]). These solutions are not mandatory; however, there is still freedom in most cases to move off the road, although that comes with a requirement to meet a set of guardrails. For example, you can choose to use a different deployment platform but you are responsible for making sure things are patched and upgraded according to our patching guidelines, that every change gets logged to our change API and that logs are shipped to our log aggregation platform, etc. This group also retains a focus on providing insight into the estate.

To counterbalance the growth in complexity of our estate due to the level of autonomy teams have had, the engineering enablement group has continued to focus on governance. For example, we've taken inspiration from established processes such as Thoughtworks' Tech Radar to identify ways of mapping out the estate. These mappings allow us to identify issues such as duplication of tooling, lack of support for tooling or gaps that could be addressed by sharing knowledge between groups. This in turn ties into existing established platforms such as Biz Ops to continually keep knowledge up to date, allowing engineering enablement to better 'enable' other groups without stifling innovation.

Most of all, investing this amount of time and energy in our cloud native approach has provided the business with the right foundations to allow us to pivot and adopt new practices and technologies faster. Our future tech strategy is a lot more reliant on people and processes than technology and tools, including focusing on building more extensible and scalable products and continued improvements to how we manage the security of our estate.

Case study 2: Skyscanner (2017)

Launched in 2003 and headquartered in Scotland, Skyscanner is a global travel search site. In 2017, it had more than 50 million monthly users. Its self-built technology, which included websites such as skyscanner.com and a mobile app, supported more than 30 languages and 150 currencies. Skyscanner successfully used some highly advanced cloud native strategies in a mixed environment: it had a monolithic core system and a fast-growing range of supplementary microservices. Part of its estate was hosted on its own servers and part was in the cloud on AWS.

Skyscanner had been using containers and orchestrators in production for around two years and its new code was generally cloud native, ie microservice based, containerised and orchestrated. The decision to move towards cloud native was jointly made between the operations and development teams and their motivation was speed. The company wanted to increase its deployment frequency and velocity. 'We saw the ability to move and adapt as a strategic asset,' said Stuart Davidson, who in 2017 ran the enterprise's build and deployment teams. According to its ex-Amazon CTO at the time, Bryan Dove, Skyscanner's goal was to 'react at the speed of the internet'. His bold ambition was '10,000 releases every day' and they were moving rapidly towards achieving it.

According to Davidson, 'Back in 2014 we were making around 100 deployments a month. We adopted continuous delivery and that helped us deploy more quickly but it didn't solve all our problems – developers were still limited by which libraries and frameworks were supported in production. Moving to containerisation plus CD was the game-changer. It increased our deployment rate by a factor of 500.'

Skyscanner's goal was to achieve 'idea to user inside an afternoon' and by 2017 they had mostly achieved that. In around two years their delivery time had dropped from six to eight weeks to a few hours. In common with many early cloud native adopters, Skyscanner achieved this as an entirely internal project using off-the-shelf or self-built tooling.

Supporting thousands of microservices within a single environment involved defining some simplifying constraints. Skyscanner developed a microservice shell that provided useful standard defaults on some low-level operational behaviours, for example network interface use. It also specified contracts and mandated contract consistency for any new microservices. The key was that any constraints made the engineers' lives easier but didn't limit them: 'Batteries are included but removable.'

As already noted, the initial motivation for adopting microservices and containerisation was deployment speed. However, once it had successfully containerised, the company rapidly started to use an orchestrator in production to reduce its operating costs. 'For us,' said Davidson, 'containers were the enabler for cloud native.'

Skyscanner is an excellent example of evolving strategy:

↳ Several years previously, the team had identified their first goal as increased deployment speed and their first step was continuous delivery. To achieve this, they successfully developed a CD pipeline using TeamCity from JetBrains.
↳ They then identified environmental limitations as a bottleneck. Developers wanted to use the latest library versions, but were limited to what was currently supported in the build system and production instances. The ops team set a goal to remove this limitation by allowing developers to bundle their chosen environment into their production deployments using containerisation. As a step in this process, they moved to a more container-friendly build tool (Drone).

↳ Once they had successfully containerised, the Skyscanner team moved again. They decided to improve their resilience and reduce costs by using a container orchestrator in part of their production environment. They chose the easiest orchestrator for them to try out at the time – the newly launched Amazon Elastic Container Service (ECS). They were happy with that and it achieved the margin improvement they were looking for. As a result, they continued to extend orchestrator use in their production environment.

Having met all its goals so far, Skyscanner then began considering its next challenges, which included handling many different production environments and making microservices even smaller in order to move even faster.

Skyscanner's voyage was a continuous, iterative process and by no means easy. According to Davidson, 'The bumps and scars make you more sceptical. Many of the tools we tried did not live up to their hype.' The company had to constantly experiment and sometimes abandon one tool entirely and move to a new one as its needs changed or the tool proved inadequate for its growing scale. It correctly didn't view this as failure but as a valuable learning process that's only possible in the reduced-risk environment of the cloud.

However, according to Davidson, this learning came at a cost to his team too: 'Every migration we had to do, every time we had to make our engineers change how they were doing something, made us lose a little credibility that we knew what we were doing. As much as the engineering community in Skyscanner were awesome about this, I was always really aware of the level of change fatigue we introduced.' To make this rate of change work, several of the company's techies took the initiative to upgrade their change management skills with a course at Edinburgh Business School.

Conceptually, the move to cloud native was a positive one for Skyscanner. The developers embraced their new responsibilities to drive and test their own releases, ops no longer imposed unnecessarily restrictive environmental constraints upon the development team, and they improved their deployment speed 500-fold. However, they didn't believe their operational journey was at, or would ever reach, an end. Like their customers, their technology teams were keen to keep moving forward to new destinations.

Skyscanner revisited (2020)

Nearly three years later, in early 2020, we revisited the Skyscanner team to hear how things had moved on. Was cloud native still working out for them?

In 2017, they had operated a hybrid cloud. Their older, still monolithic, services were hosted in their own data centres. Their newer ones used a microservices architecture and were containerised and controlled in production using ECS.

What had changed? To find out, we spoke again to their senior engineering manager (at the time), Stuart Davidson.

What did 2020 look like?

In a nutshell, Skyscanner had continued to build on a cloud native approach:

- ↳ The hybrid cloud was gone, and they were 100 per cent AWS hosted.
- ↳ They had continued to work through their services, breaking down and deprecating larger monoliths and anything that was lift-and-shifted from their data centres.
- ↳ They were making very heavy use of AWS spot instances, which appear and disappear as the rental price changes. That had saved them more than 70

per cent on their cloud hosting bills and made their operations considerably greener.

↳ They had moved from GitLab to GitHub for their code repositories, which had successfully increased their deployment speed and significantly decreased operational overhead. (Although the service did cost more and had involved a very significant internal transition for their thousands of repositories.)

Stepping back, since the early days, Skyscanner's move to cloud native had been a success, but it hadn't been a painless process. Was it still all worth it?

Responsiveness

In 2017, the CTO of Skyscanner at the time had set a target of being able to deploy 10,000 code releases a day in order to drive a different approach to how the company handled change. This challenge forced the company to automate and parallelise as much of the deployment pipeline as possible, giving Skyscanner the capability to release code concurrently and at will. That allowed them to adapt quickly to changes and issues. By 2020, this approach meant they could deploy ~90k releases to production per month.

No hybrid

When we looked at the changes Skyscanner had made, the first question we asked was why did they give up their hybrid cloud approach and move entirely to AWS? Many enterprises keep their monolithic legacy systems on-prem as moving them is a major undertaking. Why did Skyscanner think it was worth it?

Davidson's answer was scalability. In the previous two years, its monthly user count had increased very significantly. Supporting that scale in its own data centres would have been a huge undertaking for Skyscanner, and it judged that operating its own infrastructure was not a key differentiator. What were differentiators? Increased global availability, improved performance and better monitoring. It was therefore more suitable for Skyscanner to put its efforts into moving its remaining servers to AWS than into upgrading its own data centres.

Where possible, Skyscanner had started by containerising its legacy services and migrating them into its AWS ECS-based management platform, which it had become expert in from years of operational experience. Anything else was 'lifted and shifted' and earmarked for future refactoring or deprecation. This process was completed by the end of 2018 and, since then, it had been gradually refactoring the shifted services to use a microservice architecture.

In 2020, Skyscanner still had a few remaining monoliths that needed to be extracted from its system. Going cloud native had always been a gradual process and it intended to keep taking the time required.

Orchestrating change

Probably the most difficult alteration Skyscanner had made since our original case study was the introduction of the powerful Kubernetes orchestrator into its platform. The process took more than two years and was eventually very successful, although it required three painstaking attempts. So, what had happened with Kubernetes and why had introducing it been so fraught?

Back in 2017, just after our first case study, Skyscanner had made its initial attempt at a Kubernetes-based runtime and deployment environment. It did not go well. The approach had many moving parts and external components. It was driven by a configuration management tool and based on the expectation of maintaining the same hosts in a cluster over a long period of time. With the release rate of Kubernetes, the company had believed that would be the least disruptive approach. Unfortunately, it had turned out to be very fragile and susceptible to problems.

For iteration two, Skyscanner simplified its set-up significantly. It removed some of the complexity and rigorously applied the policy of immutable infrastructure by pre-baking AMIs (Amazon Machine Images). Although flexibility was lost, the reduction in complexity made up for that and it reached a sufficient enough level of confidence with the platform that some of Skyscanner's critical services were migrated onto Kubernetes from ECS.

The assumption this time had been that bigger clusters were better and that there'd be significant cost savings from large clusters with a focus on multi-tenancy. Instead, it discovered the blast radius of any problems was far too significant and that the routing layer within K8s at the time struggled at the scale of cluster that Skyscanner was operating. At one point, the team installed their own border gateway protocol (BGP) route reflectors to help manage requests within the cluster.

The team decided they still wanted to keep Kubernetes rather than return to ECS, but realised they needed a new approach. They had discovered that, in an orchestrated world, clusters replace instances as the new points of failure. Cluster outages needed to be handled. The Skyscanner team therefore revisited their whole model for cluster design.

They got rid of their large clusters, which had too great a blast radius, and shifted to much smaller sets of immutable clusters they called cells. Each service on K8s was deployed in an n+2 configuration (n being the number of clusters required to provide the service, plus one for maintenance and another to ensure they had enough capacity in case of cluster outage).

The smaller clusters allowed Skyscanner to benefit from Istio, a service mesh that controlled their inter- and intra-cluster routing. 'Using Istio,' said Davidson at the time, 'combined with our use of Prometheus and Thanos means we get an incredible amount of observability, and Istio comes with so much out of the box like mTLS that the value we're getting now feels worth all the trouble we've gone to.'

The cell architecture also allowed them to set strict limits on capacity, which meant they weren't constantly trying to re-architect to squeeze more capacity in: they just added a new cell. 'We couldn't have done that without fully committing to the cloud,' said Davidson.

At long last, their Kubernetes-based platform was finally as stable as they wanted. 'It's taken a really huge effort to get to where we are and I'm always amazed that we actually have a culture where we got something wrong like this twice but were given a third shot at it,' said Davidson. 'And we're really lucky to have development teams who buy in to some of our moonshots and are willing to put up with the patience of being our early adopters. The tight feedback loop we've had is a massive part of making this a success.'

Skyscanner revisited, revisited (2023)

In 2023, we went back to visit Skyscanner again. Fortunately, Stuart Davidson was still there and he updated us on the latest instalment of their story, which might be the most interesting yet...

Skyscanner and FinOps

We last spoke to Skyscanner just before the Covid-19 lockdown and a lot of their time afterwards was spent on cost management.

Post 2020, the company had two goals: reducing their hosting bills and cutting the carbon emissions of their tech systems. Fortunately, it found both could be addressed using one catchy concept: FinOps.

Tooling and culture

FinOps is an evolving discipline focused on the financial management of operations, usually cloud operations. It's particularly important as a way to help the finance department with forecasting as compute and infrastructure moves from being a CAPEX purchase (servers in data centres) to per-minute variable OPEX costs. Skyscanner set up a FinOps team combining representatives from engineering, procurement and finance. Their aim was to streamline systems, cut waste and save money. So, what happened?

Culturally, one of the goals of FinOps is to get the data and tools required for reducing cloud spend into the hands of the people who can actually effect that change – ie developers and ops teams – and that's exactly what Skyscanner did. To allow them to allocate the costs to each development team, they replaced some of their old monitoring tools (such as CloudHealth) with CloudZero, a service Davidson could not be more effusive about. One of the first things that using CloudZero underlined for Skyscanner was that its previous plan to make greater use of spot instances (something we discussed in the previous chapter) had paid off big time.

The alignment of cost, sustainability and resilience

A spot is an instance type that uses spare cloud capacity that's available for less than the on-demand price, and spot instances are something AWS is pushing as part of its new sustainable architecture pillar. The purpose of spot instances is to increase hardware utilisation rates, which saves cloud providers money and is a key part of improving system sustainability (ie cutting the carbon emissions and embodied carbon associated with operating a software system). Ironically, however, neither cost nor sustainability were the initial drivers of Skyscanner's move to using spots as much as possible for their operations. Skyscanner's motive was resilience.

Designing for spot instances to play a major role in a system forces that system to be resilient. In a fundamental way, spot instances are an example of chaos engineering in action. A spot instance is innately ephemeral. It's cheap (approximately a 90 per cent cost discount on more reliable hosting resources). However, it might disappear at any moment, so software running on it is forced to handle that, as is any software talking to that software. It was for this reason that Skyscanner chose to make heavy use of the instance type. It had failed to anticipate how much money it would also save!

Though we can pat Skyscanner on the back for the unforeseen fiscal consequence of its resilience play, it was not the only thing FinOps did for the company. Skyscanner coupled the CloudZero service with the observability and telemetry platforms Databricks and New Relic to route data on its systems to the responsible teams, including the cost of logging itself. Those teams then acted on that data, and the result was super-efficient (and therefore lower carbon emitting) systems. Great!

So, what next for Skyscanner?

Regional strategy

Skyscanner is a highly globalised business with compute resources distributed across the world. It pays close attention to geopolitical tensions because one often under-estimated issue with cloud native is that to use it optimally, you need to factor in global politics.

There are always international issues that affect data centre costs, availability and sustainability targets in different regions. Currently, these include:

↳   war
↳   microchip availability
↳   electricity costs and green power
↳   data privacy regulations.

To serve users all over the world, you have to know what's going on in the world. As Davidson says, 'You need a regional strategy in cloud native.'

Evolving and tuning that strategy is the next cloud native job for Skyscanner. Again, we wish them bon voyage.

Case study 3: Starling Bank (2018)

Starling Bank was founded in 2014. Based in London, it has been licensed and operating since July 2016. The bank is a successful part of the British fintech scene, which is a spin-off from the UK's strong financial services sector.

Starling is a mobile-only, challenger bank that describes itself as a 'tech business with a banking licence'. It provides a full service current account solely accessed from Android and iOS mobile devices.

It received a $70 million investment in early 2016 and created its core infrastructure on Amazon Web Services (AWS) inside just 12 months. Its founding CTO Greg Hawkins liked to say, 'We built a bank in a year.'

In 2018, Starling's tech comprised a cloud-hosted back-end system talking to apps on users' mobile phones and third-party services. As well as a full current account, the bank provided MasterCard debit cards (customers spend money on their Starling debit card and the authorisations and debits arrive at Starling servers through third-party systems). It also supported direct debits, standing orders and faster payments, which were again provided by back-end integrations with other third-party systems.

In common with everyone we interviewed for this series of case studies, Starling used a microservices architecture of independent services interacting via clearly defined APIs. As of 2018, Starling had approximately 20 Java microservices, although that number was expected to increase.

Many companies architect their services for division by tech team, ie applying a Conway's law approach, where each team looks after one or more dedicated microservices. However, like the *FT*, Starling chose not to do that initially. Instead, services were divided by functional responsibility rather than team and every service could be worked on by multiple teams. Hawkins said, 'We're taking advantage of the flexibility we get from our small size: we can reconfigure ourselves very quickly.' He recognised, though, that as the bank continued to grow, it would lose some of that flexibility: 'It won't last forever', and would then probably adopt smaller microservices and a more Conway-like model.

In terms of deployment and operations, while services *could* be deployed individually, for convenience, Starling usually used a simultaneous deployment approach where all services in the back end were deployed at once. This was a trade-off that evolved between minimising the small amount of overhead around releases and keeping up release frequency. The bank built a rudimentary orchestrator to drive rolling deployments based on version number changes. It helped to scale up AWS, create new services on the new instances, expose those new services instead of the old ones, turn off the old ones and scale down its AWS instances.

In 2018, Starling generally redeployed the whole estate four to five times per day to production. New functionality reached productions rapidly, and it was business as usual to apply security patches fast when necessary.

As always, API management was a challenge for frequent deployments. Simultaneous deployment could make that easier as both sides of the API are deployed at once. But this wasn't really true for Starling for several reasons:

↳ During the minutes a deployment took to roll across all the servers, services were inevitably at different versions.

↳ Any individual service might fail to deploy, leaving mismatching versions in production.

↳ Starling didn't *mandate* simultaneous deployment. The bank retained the ability to deploy services individually. Simultaneous deployment was a convenience that would likely change as the organisation grew.

The system had to handle all of this safely, which meant clients and services had to incorporate backwards API compatibility. To ensure this, part of the release process was validation that there were no breaking API changes (this was straightforward to check using the Swagger tool combined with the fact that client-side calls were in isolated 'connector' libraries). As the system size increased, the bank started introducing microservice-testing tool Pact to help.

From the start, the bank used Docker containers as a packaging format and EC2 instances as their 'units of isolation' (ie to separate one running service from another). It didn't use containers as the primary form of isolation, although it did use them to isolate some specific processes such as components of the monitoring application Prometheus. It also didn't use an off-the-shelf orchestrator. However, it was looking closely at Kubernetes.

Specifically, it was interested in:

↳ the abstraction it provided to machines and applications, which helped with portability (going cross-cloud)
↳ the cost savings and improved performance it would get from using containers as its units of application isolation and running on larger VM instances
↳ the sophisticated additional deployment options that Kubernetes provided.

Starling had made a strategic decision not to take on the operational overhead of managing Kubernetes itself on AWS, but it was closely watching the progress of AWS's managed K8s service (EKS) and intended to use that in the future if it reached the required level of functionality and stability.

Starling's infrastructure was entirely hosted on Amazon

and the team were happy there. However, regulatory requirements and commercial considerations meant the bank would need to diversify into cross-cloud in the future. It was therefore beginning to work with Google Cloud too, but that had a few interesting challenges: Google Cloud was, and remains, more advanced than AWS in some areas but way behind in others:

- ↳ Google's managed Kubernetes service, GKE, is much better than EKS.
- ↳ Starling had built a lot of custom advanced security features such as temporary privilege raising on top of AWS's strong APIs that would need to be re-implemented for Google.

Like any company choosing to use multiple cloud vendors, Starling would need to balance the value of consistent operations against the desire to get the best out of each cloud.

Stack-wise, Starling was a Java house. The teams at Starling:

- ↳ deployed their 20 Java services with an embedded web server inside Docker containers
- ↳ configured their estate using AWS CloudFormation plus home-grown scripting
- ↳ made heavy use of the NGINX load balancer and elastic load balancing (ELB)
- ↳ used an ELK (Elasticsearch, Logstash, Kibana) stack for logging and Grafana and Prometheus for monitoring
- ↳ used Java for Android and Swift for iOS to build their mobile applications.

Unsurprisingly, given the nature of its business, security and data integrity were (and remain) the highest priorities. The bank sensibly made extensive use of service isolation at the network level (aka 'microsegmentation'), for which they used separate virtual private clouds (VPCs) as well as subnets. All data in transit and at rest was encrypted, and inter-service communication was via encrypted RESTful interfaces. There was also a strong focus on user device security. Specifically:

- ↳ the teams guaranteed that they were always talking to the correct, original device (achieved through private keys)
- ↳ they were careful to ensure the device had not been compromised. This was why, for example, you couldn't run their apps on jailbroken devices.

Starling offered user-facing services that were latency sensitive. However, its own back end was seldom the performance bottleneck for those services. Card transactions, for example, passed through several layers of third-party systems before reaching the bank's servers, and Starling's systems generally introduced less than 5 per cent of the latency on these performance-sensitive operations.

So, Starling's back-end performance would've had to be severely impacted before it was noticeable by end users. It could therefore afford to optimise its architecture for robustness, simplicity, auditing and data integrity rather than super-speed.

This high need for resilience and auditing, and the slightly lower requirement for operational performance, influenced the bank's decision to use asynchronous APIs between its services. Each service had its own in-built asynchronous inbound command bus (a kind of queue) backed by a database. This architecture provided reliable message passing, rigorous decoupling, resilience, auditability and replayability as well as better understand-ability for the system. Given the bank's operational priorities, asynchronous APIs were a sensible choice.

From a testing perspective, Starling Bank embraced chaos engineering from a very early stage.

In 2018, Starling was very happy with the architectural choices it had made so far. Again, this demonstrated that not everyone needs to or should make identical decisions.

↪ It had chosen not to use a fully fledged orchestrator in production – yet. The bank judged that while it cost money in hosting, it made its operations simpler. Once AWS released a stable EKS, Starling planned to use managed Kubernetes on AWS. That was a perfectly sensible approach that worked well.

↪ The bank had chosen async over synchronous inter-service comms because it prioritised auditability and reliability over hyper-performance. Again, it weighed the trade-offs and made a decision based on a good understanding of its own current situation and needs.

Its original motivation for hosting in the cloud was that Hawkins anticipated it would help Starling move faster. He felt that infrastructure as a service, by supporting DevOps and an iterative approach, would help him create an innovation culture in his tech teams. That very much appeared to have paid off.

Overall, Starling Bank was an excellent example of the need to consider context when making architectural choices.

Starling Bank revisited (2023)

Since 2018, Starling Bank has grown, providing significantly more services, including a banking as a service offering. It also employs a lot more engineers and has been named Best British Bank four times at the British Bank Awards!

In 2023, we caught up with the former CTO, Greg Hawkins, to find out how the Starling systems had evolved over the intervening years. His answer was, 'Like Theseus's ship' (ie with all of its individual parts being replaced at different times).

Starling's modern systems are a gradual evolution upon the large microservices (Hawkins calls them 'mini services') architecture his teams adopted originally. Almost every individual component has been updated, but it was a slow and deliberate process. At no point did Hawkins and his team throw everything out and start again from scratch.

How things changed

The predictions Starling's teams made in 2018 about how their systems would progress have proved broadly correct.

In the early days, Starling's technology teams did not rigidly model Conway's law in their tech organisation structure. In particular, an individual team could support or modify multiple services. However, Hawkins and his engineers always believed that wouldn't scale for the business indefinitely. They were right. Now that the service count has increased from approximately 20 to 70–80, each of the engineering groups (teams of teams) owns a subset of those services corresponding to the area of the banking business they serve. As the bank scaled, Conway's law began to assert itself.

The development organisation has also moved away from the simple tooling the team built for themselves in the early days to more off-the-shelf commodity stuff. For example, in 2018, they were using a very basic home-grown orchestrator. They now use managed Kubernetes, including on AWS (EKS). They also replaced their simple ELK stack for logging with the more sophisticated Humio (now CrowdStrike Falcon LogScale) service.

There were three main reasons for the cultural shift towards using third-party services:

↳ The bank's own needs became more complex.
↳ Those third-party systems just got better.
↳ It reduced the operational management overhead.

In another change, at the start, the bank's internal services were very similar to one another, using homogeneous tooling and software stacks. The services themselves remain homogeneous, but the tooling and networking choices around them have become more heterogeneous. For example, they now use gRPC as well as REST.

The organisation's security model has also evolved alongside the tech industry's own evolution in this area. Vulnerability management and testing have become even more robust and the teams have, for example, introduced bills of materials to their releases to better track and manage known vulnerabilities.

They have also gone through several iterations of their infrastructure as a service approach. For example, as their systems became more complex, they abandoned CloudFormation from AWS and adopted Terraform from HashiCorp.

However, there remain clear similarities between Starling's 2023 approach and the 2018 one, and the organisation still prioritises safety, security and auditability above cool new tech. For example, the teams don't use all the bells and whistles available on Kubernetes, instead sticking to the bare minimum of functionality required for their purpose. They have also avoided the popular service mesh tools, such as Istio, that can provide useful security features for some users (like mTLS). For now, Starling prefers to handle security concerns, retries and so on, in service themselves rather than trusting them to a third-party application.

Overall, the culture of Starling Bank appears to have remained the same. The company balances the tightrope of providing a genuinely revolutionary service with behaving in a deliberate and careful fashion because it is, after all, a bank.

Case study 4: cinch (2023)

Launched in 2019, just before the start of the Covid-19 crisis, cinch is a fast-growing site for consumers to find, buy and sell used cars. The business's arrival was well timed and has become one of the UK's most successful ever start-ups.

The team at cinch pursued a cloud native approach from the start. However, they made some surprising moves along the way, including a screeching handbrake turn on their initial technology choice.

Why?

Fast manoeuvring

Initially, cinch went live with an uncontroversial (at the time) approach for a scalable website: running on Azure and based on containerised microservices controlled by managed Kubernetes (using Azure's AKS service). As Apostolis Apostolidis (Toli), cinch's head of engineering practice, told us, 'The site worked.'

It was an instant success, and most businesses would have been ecstatic with that. Not cinch, though. It began with one valid cloud native approach, but changed lanes to a very different one. That was somewhat of a bold move. It must have had a very good reason.

As a start-up operating in a completely new business sector in the UK (online car sales in an industry dominated by physical showrooms and visceral appeal), one of cinch's key requirements was to be able to observe the business and its hoped-for customers to learn from their behaviour. The company soon discovered problems with that, and in response did something truly scary. Less than a year into a new business, it threw away its perfectly operational website and started again from scratch. So, what did cinch replace its Azure and AKS system with and why?

The new engine

The answer was, it moved to serverless. The tech team at cinch shifted their whole system to a new cloud (AWS) and a new paradigm. They rebuilt on entirely serverless AWS services: Lambda, NoSQL databases (DynamoDB), an event-driven architecture using EventBridge and a separate observability platform (Datadog).

'By pivoting away from AKS,' said Toli, 'we were moving

away from servers, VMs, K8s and containers. We didn't own a single "host" or container artefact in AWS. To upload the code to Lambda, we zipped it up and uploaded it to AWS. We then "just used" the other services: DynamoDB [NoSQL database], EventBridge [event broker], SQS [queueing], SNS [notifications – emails, SMS], S3 [storage for front-end code and assets] and CloudFront [edge compute].

'My point here is that we didn't have to worry about the uptime or scalability of any of these services; we just used them and trusted that they would work for us. We fitted our architecture patterns around the services that we had available.'

The team coupled serverless with a decision to use third-party tools wherever possible ('buy not build') in pursuit of a frictionless system with no more technical bottlenecks.

How did it work out for them?

According to Toli, 'The original reason we switched gears from K8s to serverless was that we changed focus from B2B to B2C. This would mean:

1. **Significantly more traffic**: K8s would be resilient but serverless was deemed to be better.
2. **Spikes in traffic due to TV adverts**: So we needed elasticity in terms of performance (and cost management).
3. **We wanted to optimise for flow**: We wanted teams to iterate and experiment without dependencies. Ideally, they should own the entire stack and not rely on other teams for critical things like IaC [infrastructure as code], pipelines or observability.

'During one upgrade of K8s we brought the website down and the reason was mainly that we didn't understand K8s in Azure well enough, IaC was complex and we had to understand too much about the platform to support it.

'Interestingly, we did try to learn the K8s concepts and terminology, but we realised we would have to have a team that would help other teams use K8s effectively.

With serverless, we didn't need this team past the first few weeks – there was a small virtual team that set up all the IaC for AWS accounts, permissions, etc. Plus, teams faced less cognitive load to learn serverless than they would with K8s and, critically, they could self-serve. Literally, they were deploying code to AWS from the first week. It was then more a case of establishing the architectural patterns for Lambda, event-driven architecture and data storage in DynamoDB.'

The company had chosen a highly decoupled system and ditched most of its need for a specialised platform team by moving to serverless. Effectively, it had delegated its platform to AWS. This successfully removed the main roadblocks impeding its development speed but was not the only value serverless brought to the business.

In common with many ecommerce sites, cinch had variable traffic loads. After a TV advert went live or an event took place, there was a huge peak in traffic. The site needed elasticity and, with its fast autoscaling, Lambda was ideal for that; cinch sometimes found that the site responded more quickly under load than it did normally.

Stop, look, think

The company is obsessed with observability, and at the time of writing the product engineering teams are each responsible for their own systems. The teams use the service Datadog, which they consider an 'observability platform'. They use it not just for its monitoring capabilities but also for querying telemetry data and sharing it via dashboards, notebooks, links, etc. Toli told us that they 'go to Datadog to understand the systems and AWS to change them'.

However, it hasn't been an easy drive on a sunny afternoon.

The teams created a wide range of business dashboards and team rituals around reviewing them. For example, some review theirs every day in their stand-ups. However, as Toli points out, 'Observability doesn't happen for free. Just because you use serverless doesn't mean your systems will be easy to monitor and review. That takes effort, enablement and leadership. From a cost perspective, it costs more to understand the system than to operate it.'

The knocks

The combination of serverless and an event-driven architectural (EDA) model is not that common – but it is a very sustainable/high-efficiency approach, and AWS is pushing it hard for that reason. According to Toli, 'It was even more uncommon when we decided to go all in with serverless and EDA. AWS EventBridge, the serverless event broker we used, only launched in 2019. We decided to pivot to it in March 2020.'

However, cinch didn't choose to (and realistically could not) limit itself to only hiring developers already familiar with that paradigm, so new engineers had to be ramped up. Toli told us, 'What helped us in the early days was to mob on approaches, first across teams and then within individual teams. We would pair or mob on coding the solution so that we went on the steep learning curve together. This was critical at the start. It also helped with onboarding as literally everyone was new at cinch. Later on, we built a back-end template to serve as a start-up project for serverless back-end components.'

Another of the innovative ways in which the team handled education was to build an online coffee ordering service! According to Toli, 'cinch brew' is an observability blueprint. It serves as an example of good practice for serverless observability.

The team were very happy with their new event-driven architecture. 'What was interesting in the early days was that because EventBridge was so easy to just use, we didn't have to think about implementation details when it came to publishing or consuming events. Instead, teams ended up talking to each other about events that represented business events. There wasn't much talk about AFIs, databases, etc.

We were talking about events, domains, business metrics on our observability dashboards. Technology didn't get in the way!'

Teams

According to Toli, 'Everyone at cinch was new, and collaborative approaches like pairing, ensemble programming and working groups were cinch's way of making sure that everyone was a passenger on the high-speed journey we were on as a company.'

He's a fan of the excellent book *Team Topologies,* and one of the most interesting things about cinch is the deep thought the tech organisation has put into its team structures.

The company's approach was, in *Team Topologies*-speak, to create 'stream-aligned' teams, which were aligned with a specific problem space, eg search, inventory, finance, and were led by the duo of tech lead and product owner. This incentivised focus on product engineering and autonomy, but also accountability for the software that they, the teams, built: from IaC, application code, pipelines, and all the way to observability and SRE [site reliability engineering]. 'We had no QAs [quality assurance] at all,' said Toli. 'No ops people, no DBAs [database engineers] and no infrastructure people.'

That worked very well, but as time progressed, the company realised it also needed people who personally owned the quality of their engineering practices, so it started to assign engineers whose responsibility was to make sure things kept getting better.

Toli explained, 'Initially, we started with the embedded model: software engineers with expertise in automation and a DevOps mindset who were members of each team. It was their job to advocate and help implement things like IaC, CI/CD, observability, SRE. They acted as enablers, coaches and mentors: a catalyst and a guarantee that these things would be prioritised.'

Two years later, cinch was forced to evolve this approach

to one in which these engineers were shared. Toli said, 'We could not scale the approach of embedded automation engineers due to scale and budget restrictions. At this point cinch had 20-plus teams, and hiring these automation engineers was really hard too.' According to Toli, 'Hiring internally was a lot easier than hiring externally. When internal people saw the role, it was attractive. But externally, it was harder to articulate and persuade people, as it was often confused with infra/ops/DevOps engineers or test automation engineers.'

MOT

The cinch set-up demonstrates several things:

↳ There isn't one magic cloud native approach that suits all businesses: cinch threw away Kubernetes and adopted serverless. It chose Azure then moved to AWS. This also demonstrates that, with cloud native, companies often don't get things right the first time.

↳ For a new business in particular, responsiveness matters, and a decoupled architecture can remove bottlenecks and constraints.

↳ Cloud native is still relatively new, and cinch had to come up with some innovative ways to onboard and train new engineers.

↳ Cloud autoscaling is a killer feature for some businesses, especially ecommerce.

↳ Toli and his team rejected Conway's law and its impact on the flow of innovation. Perhaps, however, that wasn't as radical as it sounds. Although both Starling Bank and the *FT* now structure their tech orgs with Conway's law in mind, at the start they didn't. They only moved to a Conway's law approach after years of gaining an understanding of their own offering. To begin with, they did exactly as cinch decided to do:

kept themselves nimble by using cross-functional teams.

So far, the cloud native team at cinch seems to be motoring.

Do these case studies tell us anything?

OK, we've just looked at five case studies. Stepping back, is there anything we can learn from comparing and contrasting them?

Technically

Everyone we interviewed used the public cloud and gradually moved away from their own home-grown data centres. None of them regrets that; in fact, they all seem to be moving further towards the cloud and seeking out more managed services to take the load off their engineers. No one appeared unduly worried about lock-in. While, at the time of writing, the idea of 'repatriation' is in the news again, we're only aware of a couple of companies that have done this at any sort of scale.

Everyone cited increased development speed as their prime motivator. Everyone mentioned the importance of cost but it was secondary to speed and resilience.

Everyone had a CI/CD pipeline and automated tests to increase development speed.

Everyone had adopted a microservice-like architecture at least in part of production, again to increase development speed. They were happy with that decision and would continue to build new stuff with the microservice model.

Several companies' monolithic hearts had not gone away but were much less actively developed.

Not everyone had adopted containers, but everyone who had was pleased with them and had subsequently adopted, or planned to adopt, orchestrators to increase resilience and save hosting costs.

Culturally

For the *FT* and Skyscanner in particular, a cloud native approach felt like a cultural shift as much as a technical one. They both had a business-wide, ground-up objective to be agile, creative, individually autonomous and comfortable with change. They both experienced considerable pain getting into cloud native technologies so early and they both had to retool several times. However, we suspect that the difficulties themselves may have helped them with their cultural goal of building a more resilient and confident workforce.

Later entrants have an easier time. Our sector's understanding of the challenges of cloud native has improved enormously in the past few years. The Container Solutions experience suggests that companies are now getting involved with cloud native successfully without needing such a big financial or cultural investment. However, we suspect that a cultural desire for flexibility and 'radical autonomy' will always play a big part in being successful with cloud native.

10 Five common cloud native dilemmas

As we saw from the case studies, adopting cloud native still leaves you with lots of tough architectural decisions to make. In this chapter, we're going to look at some common dilemmas faced by folk implementing it.

Dilemma 1: Does size matter?

Questions we still hear all the time are 'How many microservices should I have?' or 'How big should a microservice be?' This isn't surprising – size is right there in the name – but in many ways this gets us off on the wrong foot. For one thing, how on earth do you measure size anyway? James Lewis, technical director at Thoughtworks, has been known to say that 'a microservice should be as big as my head', but how big is that, exactly? The number of lines of code would depend too much on your choice of programming language, and the number of microservices would depend on the size and complexity of your domain. Ultimately the question of size is highly conceptual.

In general, we urge you not to think about size too much.

Our judgement is that distributed systems are hard and there's lots to learn. You can buy expertise, but even if you find someone with bags of experience it might be in an architecture that doesn't match your needs. They might build something totally unsuited to your business.

As you have more services, the complexity of your system will increase, and your team will have to learn new skills, and perhaps also new technology, in order to cope.

The upshot is that your team's going to have to do lots of on-the-job learning. Start small with a modest number of microservices. Take small steps. A common model is one microservice per team, and that's not a bad way to start. You get the benefit of deployments that don't cross team boundaries, but it restricts proliferation until you've got your heads round it. As you build field expertise, you can move to a more advanced distributed architecture with more microservices. We like the model of gradually breaking down services further as needed to avoid development conflicts.

Dilemma 2: Freedom or constraints?

The benefit of small microservices is that they're specialised and decoupled, which leads to faster deployment. However, there's also cost in the difficulty of managing a complex distributed system and many diverse stacks in production. Diversity is not without issues.

The big players mitigate this complexity by accepting some operational constraints and creating commonality across their microservices. Netflix used to use their Hystrix as a common connectivity library for their microservices (although evolved to other products). Service meshes such as Linkerd from Buoyant serve a similar purpose of providing commonality, as do Istio from Google, Lyft's Envoy and Cilium from Isovalent. Some companies that used containerisation to remove all environmental constraints from developers have begun reintroducing recommended configurations, to avoid fixing the same problem in 20 different stacks.

Our judgement is that this is perfectly sensible. Help your developers use common operational tools where there's benefit from consistency. Useful constraints free us from dull interoperability debugging.

Dilemma 3: What does success look like anyway?

Moving fast means quickly assessing if the new world is better than the old one. Devs must know what success looks like for a code deployment; for example, better conversions, lower hosting costs or faster response times.

Ideally, all key metrics would be automatically monitored for every deployment. Any change may have an unforeseen negative consequence (faster response times but lower conversions), or an unexpected positive one (it fails to cut hosting costs but does improve conversion). You need to spot either.

If checking is manual, that becomes the bottleneck in your fast process. So, assessing success is another thing that eventually needs to be encoded. At the moment, however, there's no winning product to do metric monitoring, observability or A/B testing. All are highly context dependent, and in the case of observability, continue to evolve quickly, so while tools like Honeycomb may currently be leading the way for observability tooling for microservices, we expect this space to continue to see a lot of churn.

Dilemma 4: Buy, hire or train?

If you want feature velocity, then a valuable engineer is one who knows your product and users and makes good judgements about changes.

At the extreme end, devs might make changes based only on very high-level directions (ex-CTO of Skyscanner Bryan Dove called this 'radical autonomy'). Training existing staff is particularly important in this fast-iteration world. If you go for radical autonomy, then devs will be making decisions and acting on them. They'll need to understand your business as well as your tech.

People can be bought or hired with skills in a particular tool, but you may need to change that tool. Your hard skills requirements will alter. You'll need engineers with the soft skills that support getting new hard skills (people who can listen, learn and make their own judgements). In the cloud native world, a constructive attitude and thinking skills are much more important than familiarity with any one tool or language. You need to feel that new tools can be adopted as your situation evolves.

Dilemma 5: Serverless or microservice?

Serverless, aka function as a service (like AWS Lambda, Google Cloud Functions or Azure Functions), sounds like the ultimate destiny of a stateless microservice, right? If a microservice doesn't need to talk directly with a local database (it's stateless), then surely it could be implemented as a function as a service?

So, why not just do that and let someone else worry about server scaling, backups, upgrades, patches and monitoring? You'd still need to use stateful products such as queues or databases for handling your data, but they too could be managed services provided by your cloud provider. Then you'd have no servers to worry about. This world has a high degree of lock-in (con) but little or no ops work (pro).

That's pretty attractive. Most people are trying to reduce their ops work. Serverless plus managed stateful services could do that.

When the first version of this book came out, it was still early days for functions as a service, and there was a significant issue with this managed world, which was the lack of strong tooling. In the same way that Western civilisation rests on the dull bedrock of effective sanitation, modern software development depends on the hygiene factors of code management, monitoring and deployment tools. With serverless, you still needed the plumbing of automated testing and delivery.

To find out more about the current situation, we spoke again to Toli from cinch. He told us, 'There is indeed a lack of strong tooling, but it has come a long way in the past three years. With the emergence of things like AWS CDK, blurring the lines between application code and infrastructure code, a low barrier for entry for pipeline products like GitHub Actions, it's just there! You can just build a workflow in YAML. Testing is not impacted as much – it's pretty much the same as the container world. In our experience at cinch, the "plumbing" was indeed an issue, but that was mostly resolved when we started gaining experience and building templates. We wouldn't say this would be an issue for us to choose the toolchain, given the power of the "self-serve" serverless offer. It's not only about Lambda or Azure Functions; it's the event brokers and queue services, the databases that are all "just there" to be used by the teams. There's a strong self-serve aspect that helps teams write code that allows them to optimise for their business metrics rather than get distracted by technology. I'd go as far as saying that serverless enables teams to write architectures as code.'

Toli is certainly convinced by his decision to go serverless at cinch, and from a sustainability perspective, we like its potential hardware utilisation rates. It's a green choice. It's good that it sounds like it may now be a practical one as well.

11 Security and microservices

This chapter is the result of an interview with the brilliant Sam Newman, author of *Building Microservices* (2015), during which we discussed the unique challenges of securing cloud native systems and microservice architectures. Newman's book is a great read for more microservice meatiness after this book, which is a mere taster. We attribute all the intelligent thought in this chapter entirely to him.

Are microservices very secure or very insecure?

Unfortunately, the answer is 'yes to both'.

The first thing that struck us when talking to Newman was that we had written a whole chapter on microservices architecture and, indeed, a whole book on cloud native, but we hadn't once mentioned security. That wasn't because we don't care about security or it's an innate mystery to us; it's just that it didn't strike us as a big issue to talk about. How wrong we were! Of course it is! And Newman very succinctly told us why.

In a cloud native world, probably the biggest security challenge is microservices or, more accurately, how to secure a distributed system.

What are microservices again?

As Newman puts it, microservices are independently deployable processes. That means in a system of microservices you can start, stop or replace any of them at any time without breaking everything. That's great for reducing clashes between developers, increasing resilience and improving feature velocity, but for security it's a double-edged sword. It can enable you to make everything more secure with better defence in depth (hooray!), but if you don't make a significant effort it can leave you in a much more exposed position than with a monolith (damn!).

Hooray – microservices are secure!

According to Newman, security-wise, the good thing about microservices is that by dividing your system up, you can separate data and processes into 'highly sensitive or critical' and 'less sensitive' groups and put more energy, focus and expenditure into protecting your high-sensitivity and critical stuff. In the olden days of a monolith, everything was together in one place, so it all had to be highly protected (or not, as the case may be). Your eggs were all in one basket, which colloquially we tend to disapprove of, although it's not actually an unknown security strategy – Second World War Atlantic convoys successfully made use of a heavily defended single basket.

Microservices give you more opportunity to layer your defences (defence in depth) but also more opportunities to fail to do so. By now, you're probably getting the picture that this advantage isn't entirely clear cut.

Boo – microservices are insecure!

Newman also told us that the downside of microservices is that by spreading your system out over multiple containers and machines, you increase the attack surface. You have more to protect.

What kind of attack surfaces are we talking about?

⤷ More machines means more OSes to keep patched for vulnerabilities.

⤷ More containers means more images to refresh for vulnerability patches.

⤷ More inter-machine messages means more communications need to be secured against sniffing (people reading your stuff on the wire) or changing the message payload (man-in-the-midcle attacks).

⤷ More service-to-service comms means more opportunity for bad players to start talking to your services masquerading as you.

Basically, microservices are powerful but also hard to build. They can improve your security, but without careful thought they will probably reduce it. In Newman's correct judgement, microservice security needs to be considered and planned in from the start.

OK, so what should we do about it?

Identify, protect, detect, respond, recover

According to Newman (who got it from the US National Institute of Standards and Technology's five functions of cybersecurity) a useful way to think about security is as a five-step process:

↳ identify
↳ protect
↳ detect
↳ respond
↳ recover.

1. Identify

Security is expensive. There's no point wasting your time and effort stabbing around in the dark, attempting to skewer an adversary who's attacking somewhere else entirely. According to Newman (and NIST), you need to understand what you have that needs to be protected and what the risks are, and the first step in securing a system is threat modelling.

Threat modelling

The process of threat modelling helps you analyse potential points of weakness or likely attacks that your distributed microservice system will have to withstand.

One useful technique for threat modelling is thinking up 'attack trees' that cover every (often multi-step) way in which a baddie could possibly attack your system and then putting a cost/difficulty against each attack.

For example, breaking into a house. The lowest-cost way in for the attacker would be to climb through an open window (easy). The highest-cost way might be fighting the sabre-toothed tiger on the doorstep (hard).

The idea is not to make every attack impossible but to make every attack too costly. Apparently, the sabre-toothed tiger was complete overkill; we just need to remember to close the windows.

Some attacks are physical (such as breaking a window) and some are social (such as persuading someone to let you in to read a meter). The first you usually battle with tools and code, the second with processes.

The modern approach to good security is called 'defence in depth', which is a fancy way of saying don't just rely on one barrier, use several. It was the same principle often employed during the Covid-19 pandemic. If you want to avoid a deadly virus, wear a mask *and* stand ten feet away, because no matter how good a single precaution is, it's always better to use more than one and make sure those precautions are actually independent.

Finally, before starting to look at complicated security tools or concepts such as zero trust or encryption, remember that most attacks are simple. They target the open window of an easily identified unpatched system or an unchanged default password. Close those openings first.

2. Protect

So, which tools does Newman say you have that can secure the microservices and other systems you have identified to be at risk?

Encryption

Just because a connection is inside your system perimeter, that doesn't mean you can assume it's safe from snooping. Inside your internal network, the amount of inter-microservice trust you extend is a choice. You can go from *implicit trust* (ie trust everyone!) to *zero trust* (trust no one!), but the likelihood is you'll be somewhere in between.

The first and easiest tool in your toolbox is often HTTPS. If any of your microservices communicate over HTTP and you need them to be safer, you could move them to HTTPS. Using HTTPS verifies that the data hasn't been read or tampered with and verifies the callee, but the trouble is, it doesn't verify the caller. HTTPS is therefore not a zero-trust technology.

For zero trust you'll need client-side authorisation as well, which is called mutual TLS, and public cloud vendors have solutions that can help with it. Mutual TLS is also one of the killer use cases for a service mesh (unless you're a bank like Starling, which prefers to handle that itself).

If you're using other forms of communication than REST/ HTTP, then there are ways to secure that too, but it's too complicated for this chapter, so you'll have to read more of Newman's work to find out about that.

Authentication and authorisation

That covers service-to-service authentication, but what about user auth? What's a specific individual user allowed to do within the perimeter of your product? You still need to use OAuth or equivalent to cover that. You'll also have to consider whether or not services further downstream need to revalidate what a logged-in user can do, or at least verify their authority to perform a task. JSON Web Tokens (JWTs) are often used as a way to send user credentials to microservices so they can make such local authorisation decisions. Again, Newman explains this in more detail in the security chapter of the second edition of his book *Building Microservices*.

Networking

You might also want to use SDN/network security and policy enforcement to make sure traffic only ever comes at your services from other services they're allowed to talk to. Defence in depth, folks! Policy *and* encryption! Project Calico is a tool that supports allowlisting of allowed inter-service routes, although it isn't easy. Network policy is tricky stuff.

Patching

Everyone's security 'open window' is usually patching. You've got to keep all your machines and containers patched for vulnerabilities. In a microservice environment, you're probably going to end up with too many units to do this manually: you'll quickly need to automate the process. Look at tools that can help you do so, such as those from Aqua or Snyk.

Polyglot?

Microservices lend themselves to a best-of-breed or polyglot approach where everyone runs their dream stack. That has security advantages and disadvantages. Commonality is easier to secure until you've got your head around everything and automated lots of it. Keeping five stacks secure and patched is easier than 500. The benefit of diversity, however, is if hackers do find an exploit then maybe they can take it less far, just compromising one microservice. Pros and cons abound but Newman recommends that you start with a smaller number of stacks and patch them carefully.

3. Detect

Write logs and keep them for a very long time. Newman points out that the usual demand for logs is from developers diagnosing a field issue from maybe a few days or weeks ago. But intrusion detection might involve investigating problems from ages ago, so you need to keep logs longer. For example, look at the ELK stack: Elasticsearch, Logstash and Kibana.

IP-based security appliances or tools that detect unusual behaviour inside or at your perimeter are also very useful.

4. Respond

The success of your immediate response to an attack is less about tools and more about processes: knowing what to do and then actually doing it.

↳ Don't panic!
↳ Don't ignore it!

Have processes for acting on attack detection that are predefined, carefully thought through and tested. Don't wait until the problem occurs to work out what to do next, because in the heat of the moment you'll make mistakes.

5. Recover

This is the bread-and-butter stuff. Recovery from a security alert is actually just best practice for recovering from any disaster:

- ↪ Already have all your data backed up, in multiple locations with restore from backup tested.
- ↪ Already have your whole system re-creatable at will (ideally automated build and deploy).
- ↪ In the event of an attack, patch as necessary and then burn it all down and restore everything from scratch.

That's a lot of stuff you have to get in place in advance. Tough, but you're going to have to do it.

So, Newman's overall conclusion is that microservices are a hugely powerful tool for letting you build defence in depth, but they also give you lots more opportunities to mess up and leave a window open, so you need to think and plan.

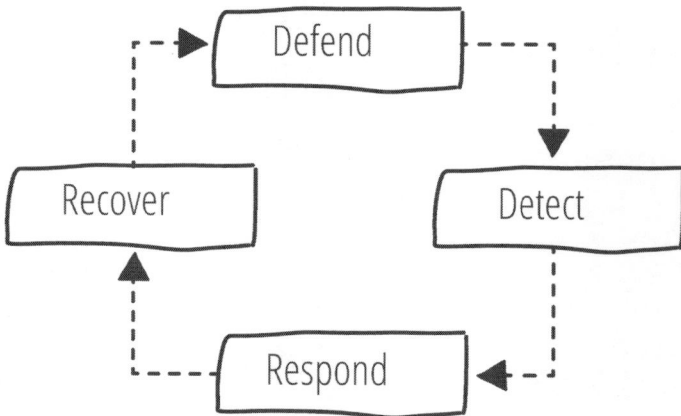

12 The state of the cloud nation?

You've almost reached the end. Well done. Just one chapter to go. Finding time to read tech books (even short ones) is surprisingly difficult!

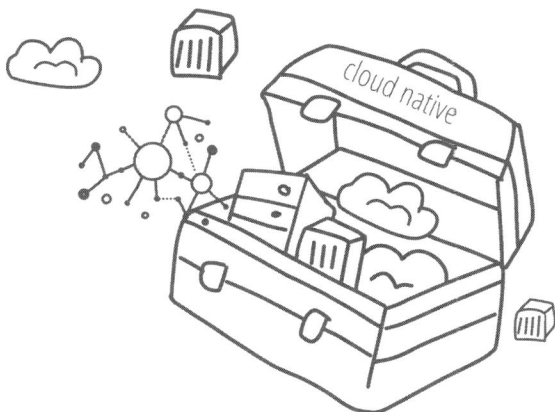

Actually, thinking about book formats can also help us take stock of cloud native. How do you 'scale up' a book? Would you scale up a book horizontally by making more copies or vertically by sizing up the text? Actually, the trade-offs (for trade-offs there are) are surprisingly analogous to those for distributed systems vs monoliths.

There are genuine difficulties with just making more

copies of a book (ie horizontal scaling). It requires more resources; there may be licensing issues; you can't be sure if anyone you gave a copy to actually read the book, how far through it they are or whether they understood it. That's the reason we don't teach kids to read by handing them a copy of a book and walking away. To share a book with young children, we choose a big font and read it together (ie vertical scaling).

Vertically sizing up text is clearly neither a fast nor a scalable approach to group reading. Usually, we distribute copies of the book. What we're saying, however, is there are always some use cases for monolithic (vertical) scaling approaches and some for distributed (horizontal) ones. Even the absurd example of vertically scaling a book by increasing the text size and reading en masse has a vital use in teaching literacy to kids. There's no one true way to solve every scaling problem.

In the introduction, we said our goal for this book was to understand cloud native: what it is, what it's being used for and whether it's actually effective. We did this by talking to companies, thinking about what they told us and considering our own experiences. We have tried to show both what we have learned and our thought processes, so the other half of this partnership (you, dear reader) can form your own judgement.

Our initial definition of cloud native came from the Cloud Native Computing Foundation, which says that, ideologically, CN systems are container-packaged, dynamically managed and microservice-oriented (or orientated if you're a Brit). We'd add another two characteristics: they need to be hosted on flexible, on-demand infrastructure (ie the cloud), and plumbed in with a high degree of automation (automated testing and continuous integration, delivery and deployment).

So, should we conclude that cloud native has a three-point checklist?

⤷ If you're containerised and orchestrated and in the cloud, but not microserviced, then are you not really cloud native?

⤷ Or, if you're microserviced, CI/CD and cloud hosted, but not containerised, then are you not genuine?

⤷ If you can't deploy 10,000 times a day, are you a cloud native failure?

Will you only win at CN if you check all the boxes? We don't believe so.

We think cloud nativeness is a spectrum, not a value system. Infrared is neither superior nor inferior to ultraviolet; there just happen to be use cases for each (inside a microwave or a nightclub, you might have a distinct preference). CN is merely a toolbox of architectural approaches that can be very effective at delivering speed (aka feature velocity), scale and reduced hosting costs. You can use some of the tools, or all of them, or none of them, depending on what you need.

For example, containers may be less useful to you on Windows servers, but you might still want to use microservices to get better dev team concurrency. Microservices are less useful to you when a quick Ruby on Rails MVP will suffice, but you might still want to containerise and orchestrate to speed up your deployments.

You don't have to adopt all of cloud native for it to be useful (although we suspect all successful CN does rely on automation of testing, code management and delivery processes).

A philosophy

Cloud native may not be a value system, but there does appear to be a philosophy to it. Everyone we met who uses CN urgently wanted to move fast and be adaptive to change in their industry, but they didn't want to break everything they already had. Their old tools and processes depended on moving slowly to manage risk, but they wanted to move quickly, so they had to use new ones. They then often used those same tools to cut their hosting bills and to scale but, critically, that was less vital to them than speed and improving their ability to respond and adapt.

We saw that cloud native was more of an attitude than a checklist. It was a rejection of the slow, visionary, utopian big bang. It was about embracing an iterative mindset, taking it one small, low-risk step at a time, but taking those steps quickly. Cloud native solutions were often distributed and scalable but that was not generally the point. The point was delivery speed: getting features out faster.

Adopting a cloud native attitude seems to mean evolving into a flexible business that embraces new technology, trusts its employees' judgement and is culturally able to move quickly, be experimental and grasp opportunities.

A cloud native attitude doesn't sound bad to us. The only question left to answer is, how can you get there as an organisation? It is to that question that we must now turn.

13 Cloud native transformations

Our other book, *Cloud Native Transformation*, is one that has been used by companies all around the world as their guidebook to becoming cloud native. It not only helps them to succeed with cloud native but in the process transforms them. They become more experimental, more iterative and seek out small risks in order to mitigate the big ones. *Cloud Native Transformation* is a companion text to this book. It features our hero, Jenny. She is a middle manager at a fictitious mid-size firm, WealthGrid.

WealthGrid faces three distinct, competitive threats. The first comes from those in its industry who have already started to adopt cloud native. By doing this, WealthGrid's competitors have already begun to win the war for both customers and engineering talent.

The second threat comes from digital upstarts like Starling Bank, which we read about earlier, that went from nothing to having a digital bank in just one year using a cloud native approach.

The third and most frightening threat, however, is the one that WealthGrid can't see coming. What will happen if one of the tech giants moves into WealthGrid's space?

These threats drove Jenny and WealthGrid to adopt

cloud native. They got it wrong twice before getting it right the third time.

WealthGrid's third try illustrates how the team at Container Solutions help their clients be successful in their own cloud native transformations. This approach has worked for enterprises in a variety of industries and, we hope, can help you too.

Three steps to risk reduction

A cloud native transformation is not just about 'moving' to the cloud. It's about combining people, processes and technology to fully exploit cloud native's advantages, making your organisation more nimble and responsive to customer needs.

When it comes to cloud native transformation, there are three steps to removing risk from the process; we call them think, design and build.

The first step, think, is all about asking questions. From questions come ideas and hypotheses, and the best of these can then be tested experimentally.

Testing experimentally is fundamental to the second step, design. Once the results of the experiments are in, they can be compared to each other and the next steps plotted.

Finally, once experimentation has taken enough risk out of the process, you can ramp up and complete the transformation. This is the third step, build, and it differs from the first two in one distinct sense: it's very expensive.

Cost and risk

Step one of our process, think, which involves coming up with questions and hypotheses, costs only time and imagination. Step two, design, for testing experimentally, has more tangible costs. Finally, step three, build, means ramping up a full cloud native transformation and is expensive, in both real and opportunity costs. Thus the time spent in the first two stages is never wasted. Unfortunately, we often see firms trying to ramp up without having spent time first in thinking and experimentation.

In the book, Jenny failed the first time because she started at the wrong end of the process; she began implementing full-scale changes immediately. This quick and bullish ramp-up was, of course, followed by an embarrassing and expensive ramp-down; she had failed to stack the odds in her favour. Let us now start at the beginning of the process and walk through what Jenny eventually did when she got this right.

Developing hypotheses

There are three common ways in which our customers start to ask the right questions:

What is cloud native? Like many others in our industry, Container Solutions provides a gamut of free, thought-provoking content, including blogs, webinars, videos, books like this one and questionnaires. We want to help people avoid the classic mistakes that Jenny made. Remember, experience is a good teacher, but it's both expensive and backward looking.

Virtual worlds: When a doctor works with their junior colleagues to help a patient, they do so in the virtual world of their imaginations. They consider potential treatments and consider their potential effects. So it is with cloud native. Using nothing more than a whiteboard, we want to ask and answer the right questions, considering what *could* happen.

The Cloud Native Maturity Matrix: As IBM Garage's Holly Cummins has argued, a cloud native transformation is as much an organisational transformation as it is a technology one; moreover, the people problems are often the hardest ones to solve. Yet organisations often focus on the technology. Our Cloud Native Maturity Matrix provides an overview of ten different axes that form part of a cloud native transformation and is a useful tool to start you thinking about what's really involved.

All of these techniques cost hardly anything and none of them ask us to write a single line of code; you can download the matrix and accompanying instructions from our website (see Bibliography).

Jenny got her cloud native transformation right when she stopped typing code and started asking the right questions. In fact, it was Jenny's discovery of the Cloud Native Maturity Matrix that helped her begin to understand the challenge ahead. Remember, experience, no matter how wise, is backward looking. The questions the Maturity Matrix poses help us to anticipate the future. Ultimately, the power of the imagination beats experience.

The Cloud Native Assessment

Those who are about to start a cloud native transformation can and do go quite far by consuming content, asking questions and considering virtual moves in the virtual world of their imaginations. In doing so, they significantly reduce the risk of the work that lies ahead. *This is (more or less) cost-free risk reduction.* No feasibility studies. No trips to Silicon Valley. Just good old-fashioned reading, dreaming and whiteboarding.

When ready, our customers move to structured thinking in the form of a Cloud Native Assessment (CNA). Although it sounds posh, in truth, a CNA is really *just a gap analysis*. The first output is a mapping on top of the Maturity Matrix, which shows where a company is and, of course, where it has to go. Here is the gap analysis from WealthGrid's Cloud Native Assessment:

Stage	WATERFALL	AGILE	CLOUD NATIVE	NEXT
CULTURE	Predictive	Iterative	Collaborative	Experimental
PROD/SERVICE DESIGN	Long-term plan	Feature driven	Data driven	All driven
TEAM	Hierarchy	Cross-functional teams	DevOps / SRE	Internal supply chains
PROCESS	Waterfall	Agile (Scrum/Kanban)	Design Thinking + Agile + Lean	Distributed, self-organized
ARCHITECTURE	Tightly coupled monolith	Client server	Microservices	Functions
MAINTENANCE	Ad-hoc monitoring	Alerting	Full observability & self-healing	Preventive ML, AI
DELIVERY	Periodic releases	Continuous Integration	Continuous Delivery	Continuous Deployment
PROVISIONING	Scripted	Config. management (Puppet/Chef/Ansible)	Orchestration (Kubernetes)	Serverless
INFRASTRUCTURE	Multiple servers	VMs (pets)	Containers/ hybrid cloud (cattle)	Edge computing

GOAL

You can see that WealthGrid was miles away from Cloud Native. The results of WealthGrid's assessment may have been shocking, but it at least gave them a dose of reality. This allowed Jenny and her team to navigate a way forward.

Cloud native transformation patterns

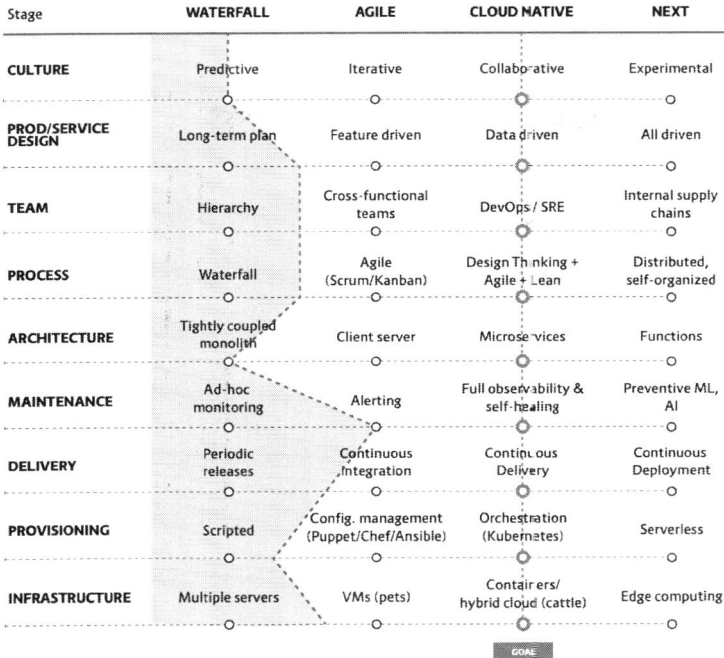

The second output of the Cloud Native Assessment is a roadmap that's made up of cloud native transformation patterns. A pattern is a known solution to a common problem. Patterns are designed by experts – in this case, by the team at Container Solutions – for use by non-expert users.

There are about 80 cloud native transformation patterns, each one captured on a card. This allows our customers to reason about effects, to consider virtual moves in a virtual world *without spending very much money*. This is known as

133

the 'design of action', which is also known as 'strategy'. Note, at this point in the process, still not a single line of code has been written nor a single virtual machine provisioned.

What did Jenny's original roadmap look like? Given the business pressures that WealthGrid faced, the first actions her company took were around strategy.

↳ **Executive commitment**: Given the scale of the transformation, WealthGrid needed to have the executives on board. This pattern is common to all successful cloud native transformations.

↳ **Business case**: WealthGrid's investment in cloud native was measured in millions. For this, a proper business case had to be prepared, which did the job of aligning the executives.

↳ **Transformation champion**: WealthGrid is a conservative company, so it needed a full-time trans- formation champion to help popularise the move to cloud native.

↳ **Value hierarchy**: Cloud native relies on distributed decision making. For example, teams are empowered to make decisions closest to the action rather than having to simply implement decisions made in the C-suite. Having a clear value h erarchy enables distributed decision making. For example, Starling Bank values security, resilience and scale *in that order*. This means that Starling's engineers can make autonomous decisions about architecture based on the value hierarchy.

A series of hypotheses

The team at WealthGrid went from thinking about cloud native, which cost them hardly anything, to some structured thinking, which didn't cost much and only took them three days. The outcome of those three days was a gap analysis, a roadmap and a set of hypotheses. In return for their efforts, WealthGrid got a significant boost in context and situational awareness and therefore a significant reduction in risk. This marks the end of step one.

Hypothesis testing

The third output of the Cloud Native Assessment is a set of hypotheses that need to be tested experimentally. These hypotheses are usually about the current skill levels of the teams, a target set of applications that might be containerised and the types of tools that might work in the company's specific context.

This experiment phase, which we call design, usually takes about 12 weeks. The goal is to learn. More specifically, when you're experimenting, you're buildirg to learn. This means, once again, certainty is increased and therefore risk is decreased.

By the time you stop experimenting, a: the end of the design phase you have significantly de-risked the cloud native transformation. At this point, companies have a good understanding of cloud native in their context, the tools that might work and their own capabilities.

Is this money and time well spent? Consider once more WealthGrid's story. Its first two mistakes cost the company a lot of money. When WealthGrid followed the process outlined here, it cost a fraction of its earlier misfires. However, this cost allowed the company to stretch its remaining budget much further. This meant that, after the design phase, rather than experience an embarrassing ramp-down, it began a steady ramp-up to the build stage and a full-scale cloud native transformation. This focused approach was cheaper and less painful. It was worth it.

Do you want to know what happened next? You'll have to read *Cloud Native Transformation*...

Glossary

Bin packing: A common scheduling strategy, which is to place containerised applications in a cluster in such a way as to try to maximise the resource utilisation in the cluster.

Cloud instance: A virtual server instance hosted on the cloud.

Cluster: The set of machines controlled by an orchestrator.

Container: A running instance of a container image. A container image gets turned into a running container by a container engine.

Container engine: A native user-space too such as Docker Engine or rkt, which executes a container image, thus turning it into a running container. The engine starts the application and tells the local machine (host) what the application is allowed to see or do on the machine. These restrictions are then actually enforced by the host's kernel. The engine also provides a standard interface for other tools to interact with the application.

Container image: A package containing an application and all the dependencies required to run it down to the operating system level. Unlike a VM image, a container image doesn't include the kernel of the operating system. A container relies on the host to provide this.

Containerise: The act of creating a container image for a particular application (effectively by encoding the commands to build or package that application).

Container orchestrator: A tool that manages all of the containers running on a cluster. For example, an orchestrator will select which machine to execute a container on and then monitor that container for its lifetime. An orchestrator may also take care of routing and service discovery or delegate these tasks to other services. Example orchestrators include Kubernetes and Nomad.

Conway's law: Programmer Melvin Conway said that 'organisations which design systems (in the broad sense used here) are constrained to produce designs which are copies of the communication structures of these organisations'. That is Conway's law.

Fault tolerance: A common orchestrator feature. In its simplest form, fault tolerance is about noticing when any replicated instance of a particular containerised application fails and starting a replacement one within the cluster. More advanced examples of fault tolerance might include graceful degradation of service or circuit breakers. Orchestrators may provide this more advanced functionality or delegate it to other services.

Microservice: A small, independent, decoupled, single-purpose application that only communicates with other applications via defined interfaces.

Monolith: A large, multipurpose application that may involve multiple processes and often (but not always) maintains internal state information that has to be saved when the application stops and reloaded when it restarts.

Replication: Running multiple copies of the same container image.

Scheduler: A service that decides which machine to execute a new container on. Many different strategies exist for making scheduling decisions. Container orchestrators generally provide a default scheduler, which can be replaced or enhanced if desired with a custom scheduler.

Service discovery: A mechanism for finding out the endpoint (eg internal IP address) of a service within a system.

State: In the context of a stateful service, state is information about the current situation of an application that cannot safely be thrown away when the application stops. Internal state may be held in many forms including entries in databases or messages on queues. For safety, the state data needs to be ultimately maintained somewhere on disk or in another permanent storage form (ie somewhere relatively slow to write to).

Stateful: An application that remembers customer state, usually on the server.

Stateless: An application that does not remember customer state.

Time to value (TTV): The elapsed time between an idea being generated and becoming a product or feature that users can see, use and pay for. One of the key reasons for cloud native.

There's a lot we haven't covered here, but hopefully this gives you the basics.

Bibliography

Introduction

The Linux Foundation (2015, updated 2023) 'Cloud Native Computing Foundation Charter'. URL: cncf.io/about/charter

Forsgen, N, Humble, J & Kim, G (2018) *Accelerate: The Science of Lean Software and DevOps: Building and scaling high performing technology organizations.* Trade Select.

Skelton, M & Pais, M (2019) *Team Topologies: Organizing business and technology teams for fast flow.* IT Revolution Press.

Reznik, P, Dobson, J, & Gienow, M (2019) *Cloud Native Transformation: Practical patterns for innovation.* O'Reilly. URL: oreilly.com/library/view/cloud-native-transformation/9781492048893

The Cloud Native Computing Foundation (2018) 'Sustaining and integrating open source technologies'. Accessed via Wayback Machine. URL: web.archive.org/web/20180329023434/https:/www.cncf.io

Noonan, A (2020) *To Microservices and Back Again* (Chapter 7), *InfoQ*, 26 May. URL: infoq.com/presentations/microservices-monolith-antipatterns

Clark, M (2021) 'Matthew Clark on the BBC's migration from LAMP to the cloud with AWS Lambda, React and CI/CD'. *InfoQ*, 29 March. URL: infoq.com/podcasts/bbc-aws-lambda-react-cicd

Kerr, J (2022) 'Jessica Kerr on observability and

Honeycomb's use of AWS Lambda for Retriever'. *InfoQ*, 2 March. URL: infoq.com/podcasts/aws-lambda-custom-database-retriever

Greenpeace (2017) 'Clicking clean: who is winning the race to build a green internet?' URL: greenpeace.de/publikationen/20170110_greenpeace_clicking_clean.pdf

Heinemeier Hanson, D (2022) 'Why we're leaving the cloud'. Hey, 19 October. URL: world.hey.com/chh/why-we-re-leaving-the-cloud-654b47e0

Chapter 2

The Linux Foundation 'Open Container Initiative'. URL: opencontainers.org.

Chapter 3

Clark, J (2014) 'EVERYTHING at Google runs in a container'. *The Register*, 23 May. URL: theregister.co.uk/2014/05/23/google_containerization_two_billion

Fairbanks, R (2017) 'Microscaling MicroBadger'. Microscaling Systems, 8 February. URL: medium.com/microscaling-systems/microscaling-microbadger-8cba7083e2a

Chapter 4

Lamport, L (1987) 'Distribution'. URL: lamport.azurewebsites.net/pubs/distributed-system.txt

Newman, S (2015) *Building Microservices*. O'Reilly.

Chapter 5

Wiseman, R (2003) 'The Luck Factor'. *The Skeptical Inquirer*, May/June. URL: richardwiseman.com/resources/The_Luck_Factor.pdf

Chapter 7

Dolgov, N (2016) 'AWS SQS for reactive serv ces'. Nikita Dolgov's technical blog, 21 March. URL: ndolgov.

blogspot.co.uk/2016/03/aws-sqs-for-reactive-services.html

Norvig, P (2014) 'Teach yourself programming in ten years'. URL: norvig.com/21-days.html#answers

Husobee (2016) 'REST v. gRPC: why we can't have nice things', 28 May. URL: husobee.github.io/golang/rest/grpc/2016/05/28/golang-rest-v-grpc.html

Netflix/SimianArmy. URL: github.com/Netflix/SimianArmy

Hof, R (2016) 'Interview: how Facebook's Project Storm heads off data center disasters'. *Forbes*, 11 September. URL: forbes.com/sites/roberthof/2016/09/11/interview-how-facebooks-project-storm-heads-off-data-center-disasters

Chapter 8

Currie, A, Hsu, S & Bergman, S (2024) *Building Green Software: A sustainable approach to software development and operations*. O'Reilly.

IEA (2023) 'Data centres and data transmission networks'. URL: iea.org/fuels-and-technologies/data-centres-networks

Our World in Data (2023) 'Electricity demand, 1990 to 2023'. URL: ourworldindata.org/grapher/electricity-demand?tab=table&country=USA~GBR~FRA~DEU~IND~BRA

Green Software Foundation 'Principles of Green Software Engineering'. URL: principles.green

Green Software Foundation 'Introduction: what is green software?' URL: learn.greensoftware.foundation/introduction

Barr, J (2015) 'Cloud computing, server utilization, & the environment'. AWS, 5 June. URL: aws.amazon.com/blogs/aws/cloud-computing-server-utilization-the-environment

Humble, C (2023) 'Podcast: Adrian Cockcroft on serverless, continuous resilience, wardley mapping, large memory systems and sustainability'. Container Solutions, 6 February. URL: blog.container-solutions.com/adrian-cockcroft-on-serverless-continuous-resilience

Pereira, R, Couto, M et al (2017) 'Energy efficiency across programming languages: how do energy, time, and memory relate?' Green Lab, 23–24 October. URL: greenlab.di.uminho.pt/wp-content/uploads/2017/10/sleFinal.pdf

Barr, J (2018) 'Firecracker – lightweight virtualization for serverless computing'. AWS, 26 Novemжer. URL: aws. amazon.com/blogs/aws/firecracker-lightweight-virtualization-for-serverless-computing

Chapter 9

Barnes, M (2021) 'Making the case for cloud only'. *FT Product & Technology*, 16 January. URL: medium.com/ft-product-technology/making-the-case-for-cloud-only-92f382ff8dd9

Thoughtworks (April 2024) 'Volume 30: Technology Radar: An opinionated guide to today's technology landscape. URL: thoughtworks.com/content/dam/thoughtworks/documents/radar/2024/04/tr_technology_radar_vol_30_en1.pdf

Babcock, C (2015) '"Cloud native": what it means, why it matters'. *Information Week*, 30 July. URL: informationweek.com/software-services/-cloud-native-what-it-means-why-it-matters

Chapter 10

Miell, I (2023) 'Cloud repatriation trends: where are we now?' Container Solutions, 9 March. URL: blog. container-solutions.com/cloud-repatriation-trends-where-are-we-now

Chapter 13

'The Container Solutions Cloud Native Maturity Matrix'. URL: info.container-solutions.com/cloud-maturity-matrix

Mueller, M. *WTF Is SRE?: The Cloud Native approach to operations.* URL: info.container-solutions.com/site-reliability-engineering-sre-wtf-ebook

Cummins, H (2021) 'No, really, cloud native is about culture, not containers'. Container Solutions, 10 January. URL: blog.container-solutions.com/cloud-native-is-about-culture-not-containers

Cnpatterns. 'Cloud Native Transformation Patterns: Tools for creating effective Cloud Native architecture – and remaking the way we work'. URL: cnpatterns.org

Acknowledgements

Anne

When Jamie first suggested a book on cloud native (and it was him!), I had no idea how long the project would continue. I just knew we were both fascinated by what cloud native was and why people were doing it. Since then, some excellent books have come out on what I came to believe was the most important aspect of being cloud native: the ability to make changes happen faster and more safely by taking smaller steps. Sometimes this is called fast flow and it is unlocked by being able to access new infrastructure on demand using the cloud. If you enjoyed *The Cloud Native Attitude*, you should take a look at *Accelerate* by Gene Kim et al and *Team Topologies* by Matthew Skelton and Manuel Pais, which is referenced in our most recent case study on cinch.

More recently, a vital reason for companies to be capable of making change has appeared and a cloud native attitude has become even more important. To handle climate change we are all going to need to evolve our software systems to run on renewable power. That's not impossible but change will be required. The ability to make it is therefore key to the energy transition, and to find out more about that, you can read my other book *Building Green Software*.

Finally, my thanks to Jamie and to Charles Humble for making *The Cloud Native Attitude* happen, particularly this third edition. Jamie always gets on board with my wild ideas and I am endlessly grateful for it! My biggest thanks, however, go to all the many folk I interviewed and have given me so much of their time over the years on this book in its three iterations. In particular: Greg Hawkins, Stuart Davidson and Sarah Wells and their colleagues past and present at Starling Bank, the *Financial Times* and Skyscanner, who have been so involved from the start! Thank you! Without your real-world experiences this book would not exist.

Jamie

The Cloud Native Attitude arose in our minds about seven years ago. At that time, outstanding books like Sam Newman's *Building Microservices* and Adrian Mouat's *Using Docker* adorned the shelves of bookshops real and virtual. None of those shelves, however, included an introduction to all the technologies and ideas that make up cloud native architectures, those wonderful microservice-oriented, container-packaged, web-scale applications that took advantage of the public cloud. With the first version of *The Cloud Native Attitude*, we simultaneously fixed that and then raised the stakes by speaking to actual companies who were moving, inch by inch, into their own cloud native futures. We did not bother to sell the book but instead gave it away. It became an unexpected hit.

The second version of *The Cloud Native Attitude* came around about the time of the pandemic. The team at Container Solutions are a social bunch who generated their sales leads at conferences. The pandemic put an end to our sales pipeline. It was thus, in the middle of the crisis, inside our highly creative walls, that version two, along with a content series called 'WTF is Cloud Native?', was born. The second version and 'WTF' were immensely popular but did not do much for our sales pipeline. We failed but we at least failed daring greatly.

As the economic winds changed in 2022 and 2023, and then continued to blow in 2024, *The Cloud Native Attitude* receded from our memories. Then something happened.

Anne had gotten herself busy with a new book, *Building Green Software*. She did that in the only way she knows how: with great vigour while bringing along and championing two up-and-coming co-authors, Sarah Hsu and Sara Bergman. Anne called me to say she'd leant on *The Cloud Native Attitude* while writing *Building Green Software*. It had held up well, she said, followed by: do you want to tidy it up and publish it? And that is how this version is now in your hands, on your Kindle or in your ears.

Almost all of my gratitude goes to Anne. She drove the initial project, used her influence to get meetings with the companies we interviewed and then did all the work of battering the copy into shape. She insists the whole idea was mine, and especially the focus on 'attitude', but she did all the work and this book would not be here without her. She continues to tirelessly educate the community and in doing so drags us all to heights we thought previously unassailable. Thanks for taking me and the team at Container Solutions with you, Anne.

The next piece of gratitude goes to Charles Humble and Jade Amic. Charles was in charge of the production of version two and Jade was leading our marketing team through the most challenging years not only of our careers but, for some of us, our lives. The highly creative walls of Container Solutions may rest on the foundations its founders laid but in those rotten years they were built by Jade, Charles, Carla Gaggini and the rest of the marketing team.

Finally, to my wife, Andrea, who held the fort in the summer of 2024 as I ate into our family's holiday time to produce this version of *The Cloud Native Attitude*. Thanks.

About the authors

Anne Currie
Anne is an industry veteran and the author of O'Reilly's new book on sustainable systems, *Building Green Software*. She loves to demonstrate that sustainability is completely aligned with the cloud best practices described in this book. She is the CEO of sustainability learning and development company Strategically Green and is a long-time friend and collaborator of Container Solutions.

Jamie Dobson
Jamie is the co-founder and first chief executive of Container Solutions. A first encounter with a BBC computer and BASIC at the age of nine launched his lifelong passion for programming and software development. Nowadays he focuses on helping executive teams to succeed with the cloud and cloud native, helping them to avoid classic mistakes.

Container Solutions
Container Solutions is a professional services firm that prides itself on helping companies migrate to cloud native. We collaborate closely with our clients, from the boardroom down, to increase independence and control and to reduce risk. We help organisations select the best path forward, regardless of vendor. We draw upon a wide range of skills honed in the real world, from formulating strategy to teaching to hardcore distributed systems delivery.